Structuring and Raising Debt & Equity for Real Estate

ROB BEARDSLEY

CONTENTS

ACKNOWLEDGMENTS

I want to thank the Lone Star Capital team for building an amazing, growing business, where we are able to learn the insights shared with you in this book. I'd like to thank my sister, Dasha Beardsley, who is on our investor relations team, for the significant help provided in editing and putting together this book. Last but not least, I'd like to thank all of our investors who entrust us to be a steward of their capital.

i

INTRODUCTION

What you're reading is a comprehensive guide to sourcing and structuring the complete capital stack for a real estate investment. The knowledge and tools outlined in this book will enable you and your team to confidently execute lucrative deals while strengthening your presence and relationships in the real estate space. Although this book focuses primarily on multifamily investments, the principles are widely applicable across all asset classes, especially as they relate to partnerships and raising capital.

The lessons and observations contained in this book are derived from my own experience working in multifamily real estate, as well as the knowledge passed on to me from other skilled sponsors and investors. As principal and co-founder of Lone Star Capital, I have evaluated thousands of opportunities using our built-from-scratch underwriting model and acquired over $300M in multifamily real estate in the last four years. This experience has allowed me to pinpoint the many factors that can make or break a real estate investment.

The three keys to any successful investment are paying the right price, structuring the deal correctly, and managing the investment well. This book aims to teach you mastery of deal structuring, which can often be the most complex element to navigate. While it's obvious that you should always pay the lowest price possible and manage the property most efficiently, the optimal deal structure is more subjective. Different investors or partnerships have varying goals, which naturally influence the design of the optimal deal structure. The dynamic nature of deals requires diverse knowledge and astute decision-making to effectively fulfill the goals of all involved parties. Acquainting yourself with the various ways to structure a deal from a debt and equity perspective will arm you with the skills and confidence to achieve the best deal for your specific real estate investment.

Even if you're a passive investor who is not actively structuring deals, this guide will be tremendously useful for vetting passive investment opportunities. A deeper understanding of debt structuring will allow you to determine whether the debt financing and equity partnership/syndication structure of a particular deal meet your criteria and align with your core values.

For sponsors, this book is an invaluable resource, as it not only teaches you the intricacies of capital structures but also explains how to find, attract, and close deals with capital providers – from lenders to family offices to syndication investors. I also walk you through the deal pitching process, strategies to create and maintain relationships through transparent investor relations, and how to avoid the major pitfalls when structuring and negotiating a deal. All in all, this book will prepare you to take on the challenges of multifamily real estate investing.

INTRO TO DEBT

Our journey begins on the debt side. In the next four chapters, you will familiarize yourself with the various types and sources of debt, determine how to structure debt effectively, and learn how to build the relationships necessary to raise debt. Debt structures may initially seem more complex because of the wide variety of options available. However, once learned, debt structuring is a relatively straightforward process to navigate. Moreover, debt relationships are often much easier to establish than equity relationships.

The first step to successful debt structuring is to acquaint yourself with the financing options available for multifamily investments. The two main types of debt are permanent and short-term financing, with a variety of loan options available within each of these categories. In this chapter, I will discuss permanent loans from government-sponsored enterprises (GSEs) and short-term bridge loans, both of which are essential tools for any multifamily investor.

Permanent Financing: Agency Loans

Permanent financing, which refers to loans with terms of five years or more, is typically the appropriate option for deals that size well based on in-place income and have a small to modest value-add component. If you're considering an acquisition of a property with below-stabilized occupancy (less than 90%) yet there is a substantial upside, then a bridge loan would be the optimal choice. I discuss bridge loans in more detail in the following section.

One of the main sources of permanent financing for multifamily investments is the government-sponsored enterprises (GSEs), Fannie Mae and Freddie Mac. Fannie/Freddie ("the agencies") provide federally backed guarantees on mortgages, making terms incredibly attractive since investors buying their bonds don't need much of a risk premium. These loans are originated and serviced on behalf of the agencies by licensed lenders, referred to as "Delegated Underwriting and Servicing (DUS) lenders" for Fannie Mae and "Seller Servicers" for Freddie Mac. While loan programs are set by the GSEs, agency lenders have considerable wiggle room when deciding how they underwrite a loan, resulting in different quotes from different lenders despite them belonging to essentially the same loan programs.

When I first started investing in multifamily, I made the mistake of assuming that all agency lenders provide the same loan terms since they all originate loans for Fannie Mae and Freddie Mac, which must approve each loan. I soon discovered that individual lenders use their discretion to determine how they underwrite deals. As a result, one lender may beat another on proceeds even if both are constrained to the same loan-to-value (LTV) and debt service coverage ratio (DSCR) metrics within the same agency lending program. This knowledge prompted me to build relationships with several agency lenders to identify those that were most willing to provide the terms I desired. These relationships have allowed my team to confidently underwrite and put deals under contract while trusting that our lenders would come through for us and not re-trade the deal at the last minute. Unequivocally, building strong relationships with agency lenders is critical to a deal's profitability and success.

Along with recognizing the variability in terms offered by agency lenders, it's important to understand how loan products and terms differ at the agency level. Although both Fannie Mae and Freddie Mac aim to provide liquidity to the housing market and support the mission of affordable housing, loan terms often differ between the two and can even differ substantially between loan products within each agency. For example, agency lenders offer both fixed-rate and floating-rate loan products, each of which may vary considerably in their terms. In my section on loan products, I delve deeper into how to successfully negotiate the best terms for fixed-rate versus floating-rate loans.

Given the complexity of the debt landscape, it's critical to not only pursue quotes from various agency lenders but to also receive feedback from both Fannie and Freddie. Consistent communication with Fannie and Freddie through DUS lenders will enable you to get the best loan terms by encouraging the agencies to compete for your business.

Short-Term Financing: Bridge Loans

Bridge loans are a valuable debt instrument for multifamily investors seeking more flexible financing. The purpose of a bridge loan is to provide short-term financing, typically for properties and business plans that are transitional in nature. For example, a bridge loan is an ideal fit (and sometimes the only option) for a property that is less than 90% occupied and requires a large capital expenditure budget. Bridge loans are most commonly provided by agency lenders through a CRE CLO (commercial real estate collateralized loan obligation) execution as well as balance sheet lenders, banks, and debt funds. These loans are almost always floating-rate and generally have higher interest rates compared to permanent financing.

It's essential to comb through every point in a bridge loan term sheet since so much can vary in the terms lenders may throw at you. With permanent loans, the focus is often on leverage, interest rate, and years of interest-only. For bridge loans, there is much more to consider. For example, in addition to the standard bad-boy carve-out guaranties required by all non-recourse lenders, bridge lenders may ask for additional personal guarantees, such as an interest reserve replenishment guaranty, construction completion guaranty, and more. Be sure to read the language of these guaranties and negotiate if they're not in line with the general market.

Another item to watch out for on bridge loans is a deposit account control agreement (DACA), commonly referred to as a lockbox. A lockbox can be soft, hard, or springing and essentially gives control over the property's bank accounts to the lender. Lockboxes, which are often cumbersome and expensive, should be avoided as much as possible. Rather than agreeing to a lockbox upfront, it's better to negotiate a springing lockbox, which is only established upon a trigger event as defined by your loan agreement. Soft and hard lockboxes, on the other hand, are established prior to closing. A soft lockbox works by having rents deposited into the lender-controlled account and then are free to be transferred to a borrower-controlled account after the debt service payment is made from the lockbox. A hard lockbox is similar but doesn't allow excess funds to be released to the borrower. Instead, excess funds remain in the lockbox to further protect the lender.

Banks providing bridge loans will often negotiate for the borrower's deposit accounts (business and personal), which can be a nonstarter for many sponsors who are not interested in establishing a brand-new banking relationship. Banks are also the most common recourse lenders in the space. Personal recourse means the loan is not only secured by the asset but also based on a personal pledge by the loan guarantors. Recourse loans range from 10% to 100% of the loan amount. For example, for a $40MM loan that is 25% recourse, the loan guarantors are personally liable for up to $10MM if the lender has to liquidate the asset for less than the loan amount. While foreclosures are relatively rare, taking on personal recourse is considered a big risk in commercial real estate, and most investors are not willing to sign recourse debt.

It's also worth checking the term sheet to ensure that interest is not charged on unfunded capital. For example, for a bridge loan with a $2MM holdback for capital expenditures ("CapEx"), you want to begin paying interest only as funds are disbursed and the CapEx budget is funded, thereby avoiding paying interest on the full $2MM from the start. Because bridge loans are short-term and often have a substantial holdback for CapEx, it's not necessarily necessary to have an ongoing replacement reserve – a monthly escrow paid to the lender that serves as savings for future CapEx. Since renovations are anticipated to be done programmatically out of the lender's CapEx holdback, it's possible to negotiate the removal of the replacement reserve escrow for a portion of or for the entire loan term and, in turn, maximize cash flow.

Another negotiation point is the index floor on a floating-rate loan. Lenders will often seek a floor on the index rate – usually the Secured Overnight Financing Rate (SOFR) – that keeps you paying the higher floor rate even when the index rate falls below the floor. For example, if SOFR today is 2.5% and a loan has a SOFR floor of 2.5%, then any reduction in SOFR in the future would not lower the interest rate for the loan. This is unfair since it forces a borrower to subsidize the lender's borrowing costs and gives the lender extra profits in a lower-rate environment. Unfortunately, my team has found it difficult to successfully negotiate floors. However, by pushing the lender to lower or eliminate the floor, you may be able to persuade lenders to instead come down slightly on their interest rate spread – the portion of the borrower's all-in interest rate on top of the index rate.

The term of the bridge loan is another important element worth negotiating. From a lender's perspective, the shorter the term the better since their capital is at risk for a shorter period of time and their fixed entry/exit fees are higher on an annual return basis. However, from the borrower's perspective, more time available on the bridge loan is undoubtedly advantageous. From my experience, borrowers often overlook this and feel comfortable with an 18-month or 2-year bridge loan because they're confident in their ability to execute their business plan. Nevertheless, having extra time is a great way to lower the risk of the business plan as well as lower the probability of paying extension fees if the loan approaches maturity before you are ready to pay it off.

LOAN PRODUCTS

Along with familiarizing yourself with the permanent and short-term financing options for multifamily investment, you should get to know the ins and outs of the two main types of loan products: fixed-rate and floating-rate loan executions. Fixed-rate loans typically have great terms and eliminate interest rate risk but are usually accompanied by severe prepayment penalties, such as yield maintenance. Floating-rate loans, on the other hand, expose you to the volatility of interest rate changes but allow for greater flexibility when selling or refinancing a property. While permanent debt offered by agencies may be fixed-rate or floating-rate, bridge loans are most often floating-rate. The following sections focus predominantly on fixed-rate and floating-rate loans as they relate to permanent financing from the agencies; however, the discussion of floating-rate debt will also be useful for borrowers seeking bridge loans. Understanding the advantages and disadvantages of each loan type, as well as how to negotiate better terms within each structure, is key to achieving the best deal, whether short-term or long-term.

Fixed-Rate Loans

An important aspect to consider when deciding whether to pursue a fixed-rate loan from an agency lender is yield maintenance – a fee paid to a lender by a borrower to pay off their loan prior to maturity. The fee is calculated based on the loan's interest rate, the prevailing risk-free rate, and the remaining term of the loan. Through yield maintenance, the lender in effect receives the equivalent of all the interest that they're missing out on from the remaining term of the loan. The severity of the prepayment penalty depends on the change in risk-free rates (10-year US treasury yield) from the time the loan was originated to when it's paid off. If risk-free rates are higher, then the prepayment penalty is lower since a lender can theoretically re-loan out the money at a higher interest rate. The opposite is true if risk-free rates have fallen since the loan's origination date.

Essentially, yield maintenance provides lenders with 100% call protection, which is why lenders prefer this prepayment penalty and will offer the best terms in this structure. This prepayment penalty only applies to fixed-rate loans since lenders are constantly exposed to market interest rates in floating-rate loans. For borrowers, yield maintenance can be extremely expensive and often prohibits them from prepaying their loan until there are around four years of term remaining or less. Moreover, yield maintenance limits flexibility in a fixed-rate loan by impacting the borrower's ability to opportunistically sell early. If a borrower is unable to pay the yield maintenance necessary to exit the loan, the property will have to be sold subject to an assumption of the existing financing, which may negatively impact the sale value.

Fixed-rate loans may also have a "step-down" prepayment structure, which is not as disadvantageous as yield maintenance, but lenders often make up for potential losses under this structure with an increased interest rate. This can still be a costly form of prepayment, given that a borrower might still have to pay 4% of the outstanding loan balance as a prepayment penalty in year four of the loan, for example.

I have rarely seen yield maintenance factored into the underwriting for a deal, which is bizarre since it can have such a significant impact on the cost and/or outcome of an investment. One rationale for this may be that borrowers often expect the deal to be sold on assumption, meaning the future buyer will assume the existing financing and the original borrower can avoid paying the prepayment penalty.

Selling a deal subject to the existing financing is an absolutely viable exit, but it's usually not without its complications. Selling on assumption usually results in selling at a discount because the underlying financing is likely less attractive than new acquisition financing since the existing debt may no longer have any interest-only payment period remaining. Furthermore, the existing debt may be at a low leverage point compared to the proposed sale price, and while a supplemental loan may be able to gross up leverage, it's still unlikely to be as attractive as new debt from a cost and leverage perspective.

Because of the potential for a reduced valuation due to a loan assumption, an investor planning to sell a property subject to the in-place debt should account for this by adjusting their exit cap rate to be slightly higher. An exit cap rate is the projected cap rate that the property will sell for in the future. The future sales price is based on the net operating income (NOI) at the time of sale divided by the exit cap rate. By raising the exit cap rate, it will factor in the lower price that the property will likely sell for due to it being a loan assumption in comparison to its free-and-clear value. Thus, while you may not have to pay any financing fees or loan prepayment penalties upon exit, there should still be some adjustment to account for the fact that the business plan is a loan assumption sale.

Floating-Rate Loans

Floating-rate debt exposes you to the risks and rewards of interest rate changes. While a fixed rate may help you sleep better at night, it limits your advantages and flexibility in situations when rates move lower or when you may want to opportunistically sell early in the loan term. Moreover, from a number's standpoint, the research shows you pay the least amount of interest when you float rather than fix over almost any period of time. For a full fixed vs. float analysis from Pensford, click here[1].

[1] See Pensford's full analysis here: https://bit.ly/pensford.

The best part about floating-rate loans from agency lenders is that they typically have a very straightforward and economical prepayment penalty of 1% of the loan amount irrespective of the term remaining on the loan. For investors who are less concerned about interest rate fluctuations and are more concerned with being able to opportunistically sell or refinance their asset with minimal penalty, floating-rate loans are presumably the best option.

Floating-rate loans can be further optimized with the sophisticated use of interest rate caps, which can have a strike (interest rate ceiling) as close to the in-place rate as necessary to protect future cash flows. Interest rate caps are used to hedge the interest rate risk associated with a floating-rate loan. Borrowers purchase caps by paying a hedge counterparty an upfront fee to set a max rate for the index rate, usually SOFR. The strike rate delineates the maximum value that the index rate can reach before the hedge counterparty begins to cover the excess interest expense. For the borrower, this effectively sets a ceiling for how much interest they could possibly pay while still allowing them to retain some exposure to the ups and downs of the floating-rate loan.

Swaps are another interest rate hedging product. Swaps give you the option to substitute a floating-rate liability with a fixed-rate payment via a hedge counterparty. However, swaps are far less common than rate caps in multifamily loans and are often only possible to execute on floating rate bank debt, not on bridge loans due to their securitization process. Rate caps differ from swaps by retaining some level of rate exposure while a swap completely removes interest rate risk.

When employing interest rate caps, borrowers generally buy a cap at the strike rate stipulated by the lender. For example, if SOFR is currently at 0.50% and the spread on the loan is 3.00%, then the all-in rate going in is 3.50%. Let's say the lender determines that they do not want the borrower to have to pay any more than an all-in rate of 5.50%. In this case, they would require the borrower to buy an interest rate cap at a strike of SOFR equaling 2.50% (2.50% SOFR + 3.00% spread = 5.50% all-in rate). Lenders typically require the initial rate cap to have a minimum term of three years and that a replacement cap continue to be in place for the life of the loan. Rate caps purchased for the loan after the initial rate cap typically must have a minimum term of 12 months.

Recently, due to the volatility of the interest rate environment, rate cap costs have gone up tremendously and are disproportionately expensive for longer-term caps. Because of this, my team has been able to persuade lenders to only require us to purchase a two-year cap, thereby keeping our costs down. Moreover, sometimes lenders do not require a cap to be purchased at all. In this case, it may make sense to either buy your own cap at your discretion or to reserve the funds (in cash) that would have been used to buy the cap to help mitigate interest rate risk in the future. This sort of decision-making comes down to risk tolerance as well as your team and your investors' views on the future of interest rates.

While lenders often have a stipulated maximum rate cap strike that you must adhere to, nothing is stopping you from purchasing a rate cap that is much closer to where the floating index rate is today. Naturally, you should analyze the cost of rate caps at various strikes to determine which is the most economic. An especially attractive option is to purchase a rate cap very close to the current index rate. Purchasing this rate cap would likely be very expensive, but in doing so, you would synthetically create a "fixed-rate" loan with a 1% prepayment penalty. To properly analyze the economic viability of this option, you should simply factor the cost of this rate cap into the "all-in" interest rate of the loan and compare this to the interest rate of an equivalent fixed-rate loan with a step-down prepayment penalty (use the proposed future sale date to calculate the cost of the step-down prepayment penalty).

One last thing to consider in this analysis is the fact that the actual higher interest rate of the fixed-rate, step-down prepayment loan option from an agency would likely result in lower proceeds since most loans today are debt service coverage ratio (DSCR) constrained. This is because the higher interest rate of the loan would negatively impact the DSCR, which typically must be 1.25x (NOI must be 125% of amortized debt service). This sort of underwriting issue does not exist for bridge loans because they are sized based on stabilized performance metrics, but most bridge loans are floating-rate loans, so they also require interest rate caps as discussed above.

STRUCTURING DEBT

Now that you understand some of the critical elements and nuances of debt financing, let's discuss how to optimally structure debt and finalize deals. The first step is to identify the property type and business plan and ensure those match the financing. For example, you shouldn't put bridge debt on a stabilized Class A property. Instead, you should opt for lower leverage debt from a life insurance company or an agency lender. Similarly, if you plan to only hold the property for 3 years, 10-year fixed-rate debt is unlikely to be a good match for your business plan due to prepayment penalties.

Matching the timing of the anticipated hold period to the debt term is essential. As mentioned above, if you're looking for flexibility or a shorter-term hold, a floating-rate loan may be the best option. Another option would be to pay an agency lender a higher interest rate in order to secure a step-down prepayment penalty rather than yield maintenance. An example of a step-down prepayment penalty would be "5,5,4,4,3,3,2,2,1,1", with each number corresponding to the prepayment penalty as a percentage of the outstanding loan balance. Evidently, even with paying the premium for a step-down prepayment penalty on a 10-year loan, it still can be quite expensive to exit in the first few years.

The next aspect to consider is the leverage of the loan as it relates to the purchase price and the total project cost. For example, if you're buying a property for $10MM but have an anticipated CapEx budget of $2MM, you're going to have to bring a whole lot of equity to the table if the CapEx budget is not financed by the loan. For this scenario, you should seek out a bridge loan, which would provide leverage based on the total project cost ($12MM), rather than a loan that only accounts for the price/appraised value and in-place cash flow. However, you should also examine whether or not the stabilized value of the property justifies the additional leverage that a bridge loan is capable of providing. Rigorous underwriting is necessary to determine the suitability of a bridge loan, including a refinance exit test, which I walk through in detail in my book, The Definitive Guide to Underwriting Multifamily Acquisitions.

If you determine that the additional leverage and shorter term associated with a bridge loan are not a good fit for your deal, you may opt for a permanent loan with a floating-rate execution. This can work similarly to a low-leverage bridge loan since you can exit the loan for just a 1% prepayment penalty. If you're keen on additional leverage but don't feel comfortable with the 18-month to 3-year term of the bridge loan, you could also pursue a 10-year floating-rate agency loan paired with a tranche of preferred equity to bring the leverage up to bridge loan levels while maintaining the 10-year maturity.

Preferred ("pref") equity is a financial instrument often used to build leveraged real estate capital structures. This unique product straddles the line between debt and equity, sharing attributes of both, and loan terms can be tailored to lean more in either direction. Legally, it's an equity investment; however, pref equity receives priority on both distributions and return of capital, subordinate only to the senior loan. It's debt-like in the sense that it's superior to common equity, earns a fixed rate of return, and has default remedies/control rights, but its pricing is more expensive, similar to equity. While senior lenders typically offer leverage of up to 70–80% of the value (LTV) of the asset, pref equity investors can bring total leverage to 80–90% of total capitalization (sum of senior loan proceeds and preferred equity investment). Most would consider this all-in leverage to bear equity-like risk, which is why pref lenders favor deals that build up property value by improving the property and operations, and proportionately bring down the pref equity's "last-dollar basis" as a percentage of the rising property value similar to a bridge loan. We will discuss preferred equity in further detail in the later chapters on equity.

RAISING DEBT

Once you have determined the best loan type and structure for your deal, you may seek out lenders and provide them with your initial loan package so they can review it and provide a quote. While this is a preliminary step of due diligence, it's still important to present the deal and your loan request in the best way possible.

The key elements to a loan package are the property financials, your pro forma/business plan, your anticipated purchase price, and your anticipated CapEx budget. In addition to these property-specific items, you will also need to provide thorough information on the sponsorship team if the lender isn't familiar with the team already. For example, the lender will want to see the company bio, know the track record of the team specifically as it relates to the deal at hand, as well as business resumes, net worth, liquidity, and real estate owned schedules (REO) of all of the key principals (KPs) signing on the loan. "Key principal" is a term used by lenders to describe loan guarantors. Typically, lenders are looking for the cumulative net worth of the KPs to be equal to the loan amount and their cumulative liquidity (cash, stocks, and bonds) to equal 10% of the loan amount. As your team's experience grows, deal sizes increase, and relationships with lenders improve, these net worth and liquidity requirements become slightly less stringent.

The most fundamental aspect of your loan package is your business plan/pro forma. Even for permanent loan requests where the lender is constrained to underwriting to in-place cash flow, supplying the right pro forma and business plan information can go a long way to getting the best loan possible. Specifically, for permanent loans, lenders must underwrite to in-place revenue, but they're also able to underwrite to pro forma expenses. Therefore, if you have a compelling case as to why/how expenses can and should be lower, including this in your pro forma can enable you to get "credit" for it towards the loan's underwritten net operating income (NOI). Certain permanent lending programs may even take into account your CapEx budget, in part or in total, in the loan amount calculation, which can help you secure additional leverage. This makes it all the more imperative to present a rough CapEx budget upfront so the lender can factor it in.

For bridge loans, your story, business plan, and budget become doubly important. Bridge lenders offer loans not based on in-place cash flow but on future cash flow and value. Just like your equity

investors, bridge lenders must believe in your
business plan and your team's ability to execute it. All
of the above materials must be presented to the
lender persuasively to get them on board with the
opportunity. In addition to the pro forma expenses as
discussed above, showing a strong pro forma revenue
justified via rental comps is necessary for the lender
to confidently underwrite a high stabilized/post-
renovation income and value.

Beyond the initial lender underwriting phase, there is
much more due diligence and proper structuring to
work through to secure the debt. You must avoid
major pitfalls that could derail the loan or cause you
to compromise the deal for yourself and/or your
team.

First, it's highly recommended to have your general
partners (GPs) team and KPs in place as early as
possible. "General partner" is used interchangeably
with sponsor, syndicator, manager, and operator, and
your GP team consists of any such individuals that
partner with you to raise capital and/or manage the
deal. As mentioned before, the KPs signing on the
loan must satisfy the lender's experience, net worth,
and liquidity requirements. Due to the rigidity of
these requirements, many sponsors, especially when
starting out, seek out a loan guarantor or co-signer to
fulfill these needs. It's best to identify and negotiate
the terms of your guarantor's role in the deal ahead of
time to avoid scrambling at the last minute or re-
trading (the cosigner changing the terms of the
agreement).

You can meet potential loan guarantors throughout the real estate space – at meet-ups, conferences, and online. Sponsors constructing their own deals may sometimes be open to co-signing on another sponsor's loan. Finding a loan guarantor is all about relationships because it's a partnership that requires significant trust. If you haven't already, start building collaborative relationships with other people in your space, even if it may seem like they're your competitors. Although it may sound cliché, real estate really is a team sport and most people in the business are willing to help each other out.

The next piece to make sure checks out is your deal's organizational structure. Every deal is different but there are two things lenders almost always check the organizational chart and operating agreement for – minimum KP investment and the major investor threshold. Typically, lenders want to see the sponsor/KPs cumulatively invest around 10% of the equity for the deal. This requirement is not as strict for larger transactions, but some meaningful KP contribution is generally desired. Make sure you plan ahead to avoid being blindsided by a co-investment requirement. Even if you have not secured a lot of capital, the deal will likely succeed if you prepare an adequate explanation for the lender in advance.

The next stipulation is the major investor threshold, which triggers a full underwriting and "know your customer" review if the lender discovers that any individual who is not a KP is going to own 20% to 25% or more of the borrowing entity. You don't want your investor or yourself to be blindsided by this so make sure to either avoid any of your investors owning more than 20% of the deal or to ensure your investor understands that their desired level of ownership will result in the lender requiring personal financial statements, a real estate owned (REO) schedule, a credit check, and other background information.

Lastly, you must coordinate proper assistance from your team, which includes your property management company, your brokers and consultants, and any other individuals involved in facilitating your side of the deal. Your property management company should put together a budget showing the leanest possible expenses for the lender. While agency lenders can only underwrite revenue to in-place numbers, they can underwrite expenses based on your budget. It's therefore critical that your property management budget pushes the lender to arrive at the strongest underwritten net cash flow possible.

Your insurance broker should scrutinize lender-proposed insurance requirements and negotiate out unneeded coverage, bringing the premium down as much as possible. This not only saves you money on expenses, but also allows the lender to underwrite lower expenses, and thus derive a higher property valuation and greater loan amount. Moreover, your property tax consultant may be able to provide an analysis that informs the underwriting process in a more accurate way than the standard assumptions. This information can make you and your lender comfortable with underwriting a lower property tax assessment moving forward.

Should you choose to use a mortgage broker, they should identify the best lender candidates that fit your deal profile and create competition between them to deliver the most advantageous loan terms. Whether you're using a broker or going directly to lenders, if you don't feel that your mortgage broker or lender is doing everything in their power to see you succeed, then it's worth finding a new lender or broker who will go the extra mile. You can find lenders by looking at the sponsors of commercial real estate events and through word of mouth from your networking relationships. If you are planning on using a loan guarantor, you can ask them to introduce you to new lenders. Working with a lender that has a strong relationship with your loan guarantor benefits and de-risks the deal.

INTRO TO EQUITY

Now that we've covered the debt side of capital structures, let's move on to the fun stuff -- equity. The equity world in commercial real estate is extremely diverse, with terms and structures varying widely. The diverse and variable nature of equity also makes it more complex to navigate, which is why I dedicate the majority of this book to the subject. The following chapters outline various equity structures, components, and tools; the principal types of equity partners/investors and their goals/preferences; strategies for measuring and achieving expected returns; and capital raising strategies for creating and maintaining investor relations. In this particular chapter, I introduce the two primary types of equity – common equity and preferred equity. Once you understand these basic types of equity, you can begin thinking about how to structure your deals to attract investors and optimize the risk versus return profile of your investments.

Common Equity

An equity investment that doesn't have seniority over other equity in a deal is called common equity. Common equity is the riskiest portion of the capital stack because it doesn't have any cushion (unlike debt and preferred equity, which have equity cushion). This means common equity sits in a "first loss" position. On the other hand, common equity benefits the most on the upside because its potential for profit is unlimited, whereas debt and pref equity earn a fixed rate of return.

In the context of a joint venture or syndication, the common equity consists of general partner (GP) equity and limited partner (LP) equity. A GP, also known as a sponsor, is responsible for finding the property, raising the debt and equity, and managing the operations, business plan, distributions, accounting, and communications. In return for these efforts, sponsors incorporate fees and are allocated performance compensation/profit participation in the deal structure.

LPs, also known as capital partners, are solely responsible for providing capital and bear no risk beyond their investment. An LP's focus and efforts lie in the sourcing of sponsors and deals, as well as conducting due diligence. Once the investment is made, a dutiful LP stays on top of the investment by reading sponsor communications, providing feedback, and keeping track of their distributions.

With an abundance of capital and a variety of sponsors and deals to choose from, being an LP is an envious job. Because LPs have so many options, sponsors must work hard to build relationships and differentiate themselves via deal sourcing, strategy, operational capabilities, reporting, deal structure, and customer service.

There are a variety of ways sponsors can structure common equity to align with LPs' interests/goals. For example, Lone Star Capital uses a multi-class common equity structure, discussed in greater detail in Chapter 6. In this structure, investors are incentivized to put down larger investment minimums in exchange for qualifying for a "higher" class and gaining preferential terms. In contrast, equity structures that incorporate preferred equity, such as the dual-tranche structure, may find it more difficult to attract certain LPs but may also present the potential for higher returns. I'll outline the pros and cons of the dual-tranche equity structure in the next chapter.

Preferred Equity

As explained previously in the section on debt structuring, preferred ("pref") equity is a bit of a hybrid between debt and equity. Like debt, pref equity has priority over common equity, earns a fixed rate of return, and has default remedies/control rights; but like common equity, it's a more expensive source of capital that remains subordinate to the senior loan. Its purpose is to provide supplemental leverage for sponsors and consistent returns for investors.

Pref equity is typically structured with a portion of the "interest" or payment requirement to be made monthly, similar to regular debt service, and with the rest of it accrued to the payoff of the pref position. An example of terms are 9% current pay (out of monthly cash flow) and 4% accrual (annual calculation) for a total of 13% simple return. However, to your advantage, pref equity can be incredibly flexible. For instance, if the property has insufficient cash flow to pay the monthly requirement, the first 6 months or year of current pay could be deferred or prepaid upfront/capitalized, relieving the cash flow strain on the property during the initial stabilization period.

Pref equity is quite similar to mezzanine ("mezz") debt, which also has characteristics of both equity and debt. Mezz loans are subordinate to senior debt but have priority over both preferred and common equity. However, the key difference between the mezz debt and pref equity lies in their legal structures. Whereas pref equity investors have direct ownership of the borrowing entity, mezz debt lenders hold a pledge of the investment's equity as collateral. If the mezz borrower defaults, then the mezz lender can obtain ownership of the pledged entity via Uniform Commercial Code (UCC) foreclosure. Since mezz debt only holds a pledge as collateral, no tax benefits flow to the mezz borrower (not all preferred equity investors require that tax benefits flow to their portion of the ownership either). In sum, both preferred equity and mezzanine financing provide supplemental financing subordinate to senior loans and have priority over common equity, as well as default remedies in the event of nonpayment.

It's not as easy to get pref equity or mezz debt behind a max leverage bridge loan because there isn't much room in the capital stack for it to fit. For example, if a lender is providing an 80% loan-to-cost (LTC) bridge loan, there may only be room for a pref equity investor to provide an additional 5% LTC – a high-risk position that may be too small in dollar terms. For this reason, pref equity and mezzanine debt can be a great fit for value-add deals that are financed with permanent senior debt or deals being acquired subject to a low-leverage loan assumption.

To clarify, pref equity is usually not the best product for deals without a value-add component since there is no business plan-driven value creation, which is key to paying off investors through a refinance. Without value creation, the pref equity investor must rely on the sale of the asset to recoup their investment.

For pref equity that provides 90%+ LTC (when combined with the senior loan), the cost becomes much more expensive, and the structure starts to look more like joint venture equity. This is because, as pref equity provides more and more of the equity for a deal, there is less and less common equity for the pref equity to subordinate, thus reducing its downside protection. Many investors view 90%+ of the capitalization as "equity risk" and, naturally, want to get paid for it. These higher leverage pref pieces are often called "participating preferred equity" since there is an equity kicker – a component of the pref structure that entitles the preferred equity investor to a portion of the upside, similar to what a common equity investor would get.

Like all leverage, preferred equity and participating preferred equity cut both ways. If the deal performs well, the return to the common equity is magnified. However, if the deal underperforms, the downside scenario is exacerbated by the added leverage. When contemplating whether to implement pref equity or participating pref equity, it's wise to evaluate the downside and stress test the deal. Furthermore, it's important to assess the returns on a risk-adjusted basis by properly factoring in the added risk of the additional leverage by way of the (participating) preferred equity. This can be challenging, given that risk is often difficult or even impossible to precisely quantify. Thus, you should rely on your best judgment and market/investor feedback to assess the viability of taking on pref equity as well as that of raising the common equity (which would then be subordinate to the pref equity).

Raising pref equity is substantially easier than common equity, but including it in your deal structure can make it significantly more difficult to attract common equity investors (LPs). Many private funds and family offices refuse to invest in common equity if it's subordinate to a slice of preferred equity, because they aren't interested in being in such a leveraged position.

The tug of war between leverage and returns puts sponsors in a difficult position. While greater leverage magnifies potential returns, thereby making the deal seem more attractive, it can also turn off or even preclude certain investors with firm leverage constraints from considering the opportunity. This dilemma underscores the importance of making sure your deal profile/business plan, capital structure, and investors are all in alignment. You should get feedback from your potential investors as to the deal profile and capital structure they're looking for to see if these match your strategy.

DUAL-TRANCHE EQUITY STRUCTURE

The dual-tranche equity structure is an incredibly useful tool for multifamily syndications. This structure slices up the equity into two groups, a preferred equity tranche and a subordinate common equity tranche. The preferred equity tranche (also known as Class A) is senior to the common equity (Class B investors) and earns a fixed rate of return (typically 9 or 10%). Essentially, Class A investors trade the upside from potentially higher cash flows or profits on sale for a more secure and stable current yield. The common equity is subordinate to the preferred equity, meaning it can only receive cash flows after the pref equity's fixed return is paid. Wrapped around this equity structure is the sponsors' or general partners' promote – performance-based compensation earned from cash flows and profits upon sale. This means the common equity may still have a preferred return, which must be paid before the general partners (GPs) earn their promote, but this preferred return is still subordinate to that of the Class A investors.

Since Class A investors do not participate in the profits upon sale, the common equity receives all of the profits upon sale, thereby increasing returns for Class B investors, assuming the deal performs at or above the Class A return rate (net of fees and promote). This senior-subordinate structure optimizes the capital stack because it lowers the project-level cost of capital by more closely aligning risk to returns. In other words, incorporating pref equity into your capital structure allows you to attract investors who are happy to accept a lower return in exchange for being in a lower-risk position in the capital stack. Additionally, the pref equity (Class A) is favorable for the sponsor because it typically does not have default remedies or a maturity date, and it can be cheaper than mezzanine financing because tax benefits usually flow to the preferred equity investors. While my team has never implemented the dual-tranche syndication structure, it can make sense for sponsors to do so if it helps them raise capital. However, it's important to note that this structure doesn't necessarily make the deal more profitable for sponsors.

At first blush, this structure may look like an attempt on the sponsors/GPs part to increase their promote. However, a deeper look is necessary to unpack the ramifications of implementing this syndication structure. It's imperative that GPs understand how this structure affects their total compensation. Many sponsors mistakenly assume that because the preferred equity acts as leverage and increases the common equity returns, it will also increase their returns. However, this is often not the case. In fact, given the low level of cash flows typically found in deals in this current market environment, this structure can actually reduce sponsor compensation.

The irony of this is that sponsors are looking to implement the dual-tranche structure precisely for deals that underwrite to lower returns, with the aim of using the structure to advertise the higher returns achieved from the leverage provided by the preferred equity. However, to fully understand how the returns are affected, you must first master positive leverage – the concept that yield increases if it's levered by a lower cost of capital. This is essentially the premise on which the entire commercial real estate business is built upon. The goal is to buy property that has an unlevered yield (cap rate) that is higher than the interest rate of the mortgage. For example, if you buy a property with a 5% cap rate and finance the acquisition with a 75% LTV mortgage with an interest rate of 4%, you have achieved positive leverage and will see your return go from 5% (cap rate/unlevered yield) to 8% (cash-on-cash/levered yield). As you can see, even a modest spread of 100 basis points (1 basis point is .01%) results in a dramatic increase in cash-on-cash returns. For deals that are purchased at low cap rates resulting in negative leverage, the goal is to increase the income of the property so that the stabilized yield on cost (NOI divided by the total project cost) is greater than the cost of debt, thus creating positive leverage down the road.

This same principle holds true for all parts of the capital stack. For instance, if the project's cash-on-cash return is 12%, but the preferred equity investors only receive a 10% fixed return, the cash-on-cash return for the common equity will increase to 14%. However, as you know, leverage cuts both ways. If the project's cash-on-cash is only 8% yet the preferred equity still gets paid 10%, the cash-on-cash will be reduced to only 6% (both scenarios assume the preferred equity and common equity are each 50% of the total equity). This is the power of positive (or negative) leverage. However, these examples only demonstrate leverage's impact on the cash-on-cash returns and not the total returns achieved after the sale – which is where the real money is made for the common equity holders. Rather than the sale profits being shared by both the common and preferred equity partners, the common equity shares in the profits along with the GP. Thus, by utilizing this structure, the common equity could essentially double the profits it would otherwise earn upon sale. And since the internal rate of return (IRR) is often greater than 10% (cost of the pref), the leverage of the preferred equity is accretive to total returns.

In sum, with the dual-tranche structure, the common equity typically receives lower cash-on-cash returns than it would otherwise, but a significantly larger profit upon sale (higher IRR) makes up for these lower cash flows. This higher IRR makes GPs happy because they're better able to sell the returns of their deal to their common equity investors as well as appease their yield-focused investors through the secure, preferred equity position. However, the monetary implications for the GP itself may not be quite as favorable.

The GP's participation in the cash flows via their promote will decrease or become nonexistent in a negative leverage scenario since the GP's promote is usually subordinated by an 8% preferred return offered to the common equity (not to be confused with preferred equity). The default assumption is that the GP would also be able to make up for these lower cash-on-cash returns with the sale, right? Actually, no. The GP's compensation via the sale remains the same in a traditional syndication or in a dual-tranche syndication. The sponsor earns 20 to 30% of the sale profits as their promote, but the sale profits do not change based on the equity's internal leverage coming from the preferred equity tranche. A sponsor can potentially make up for this by adding an IRR hurdle into the structure (e.g. the sponsor can increase the promote to 50% after an 18% IRR is delivered to the common equity, which is more feasible when the deal is levered behind the fixed-return preferred equity).

Below is an example of how the dual-tranche syndication structure can affect a sponsor's compensation in a negative leverage scenario.

Scenario #1: Traditional Syndication

In this first scenario, the sponsor is charging a 2% acquisition fee and a 2% asset management fee, is offering an 8% preferred return, and has a 30% promote. For this deal, the LP returns are 13.9% IRR and 8.4% cash-on-cash over a five-year hold. These total returns are a little light (but the cash on cash is strong) so this deal may be a bit harder to sell to investors.

Here is how the total GP compensation breaks down:

Total General Partnership Compensation							
Fees & Promotes	Year 0	Year 1	Year 2	Year 3	Year 4	Year 5	Total
Acquisition Fee	$260,000						$260,000
Loan Guarantee Fee	$0						$0
Asset Management Fee		$30,942	$34,661	$37,290	$38,349	$39,409	$180,650
Cash Flow Promote		$0	$0	$0	$1,466	$43,191	$44,657
Sale Promote				$0	$0	$954,462	$954,462
TOTAL	**$260,000**	**$30,942**	**$34,661**	**$37,290**	**$39,815**	**$1,037,062**	**$1,439,769**

Scenario #2: Dual-Tranche Syndication

Here's the same investment but with a dual-tranche structure instead of a traditional common equity structure, with one single class of equity. In this scenario, we have a 10% preferred equity tranche that makes up 50% of the equity. The LPs pay the same fees and promote to the sponsor as in the traditional syndication (see Scenario #1 above). However, here, the common equity receives a 17.1% IRR and an average cash-on-cash return of 7%. Although the cash-on-cash return went down, the IRR jumped to an impressive 17.1%, which is much more attractive than the 13.9% IRR in the previous scenario and can be a game-changer for an investor on the fence.

Here is how the GP compensation breaks down in this scenario:

Total General Partnership Compensation							
Fees & Promotes	Year 0	Year 1	Year 2	Year 3	Year 4	Year 5	Total
Acquisition Fee	$260,000	$0	$0	$0	$0	$0	$260,000
Loan Guarantee Fee	$0	$0	$0	$0	$0	$0	$0
Asset Management Fee	$0	$30,942	$34,661	$37,290	$38,349	$39,409	$180,650
Cash Flow Promote	$0	$0	$0	$0	$0	$0	$0
Sale Promote	$0	$0	$0	$0	$0	$681,296	$681,296
TOTAL	$260,000	$30,942	$34,661	$37,290	$38,349	$720,705	$1,121,946

As you can see, even though the LP returns went up
for the common equity, the sponsor is projected to
make less money because they don't hit their promote
until the sale. This is because the cash-on-cash returns
are lower due to negative leverage. The 8% preferred
return must be made up upon sale, which leads to a
significantly lower sale promote for the GP.

Needless to say, sponsors should thoroughly analyze
how their compensation is affected through the
implementation of various capital structures. In this
example, the GP is making 22% less with the dual-
tranche structure. Sponsors need to ask themselves
whether a deal is truly worth it just because it can be
structured in a way that gets their investors to bite.
Just because you can doesn't mean you should. On
the flip side, investors should model out the projected
returns for LPs and GPs and question why the
sponsor(s) is willing to reduce their returns so
dramatically, if that is the case. One potential rationale
is that the sponsor(s) is fee-focused and, thus, cares
more about executing the deal to generate acquisition
and asset management fees than optimizing the deal
to maximize promote compensation. An investor
could reasonably ask a sponsor looking to set up this
dual-tranche structure to reduce their acquisition fee
to 1% (assuming it was originally at 2%) in exchange
for increasing the promote or establishing a tier 2

return hurdle, whereby the sponsor's promote increases above a 13-18% IRR. Their response could reveal whether the interests of the sponsor(s) and the potential LPs are truly aligned.

Additionally, LPs should recognize that the higher projected returns associated with a dual-tranche structure are derived from leverage and are thus riskier. Moreover, because dual-tranche is a senior-subordinate structure, the common equity investors will bear the first principal loss in an unfavorable sale and could quickly see their cash flows evaporate in difficult times. LPs should scrutinize coverage ratios and break-even metrics when evaluating the risk of an investment. In my opinion, the leverage employed by the dual-tranche syndication structure is worth the additional risk since the preferred equity investors typically don't have control rights or default remedies unlike 3rd party preferred equity providers. All in all, this is an optimal structure for both cash flow investors and investors seeking higher total returns since each tranche (pref equity and common equity) caters well to each investor type. Investors should also keep in mind that in most scenarios where this structure is employed, the GPs are opting to make less money (whether they realize it or not).

On the bright side, investments that have project-level, levered cash flows higher than the preferred equity tranche's return (typically 10%), everybody wins. The common equity LPs will see higher projected cash-on-cash returns than they would in a traditional structure and the GP will make more money from the promote as well. My team will definitely consider employing this structure on deals where we underwrite to this positive leverage scenario. In fact, we would even consider dual-tranche syndication for certain deals resulting in negative leverage because of how nicely it caters to two very different types of investors.

ELEMENTS OF A TYPICAL EQUITY STRUCTURE

In this chapter, I'll discuss the two main components of a typical equity structure: sponsor fees and the waterfall / promote structure. These structural components will be discussed in the context of Lone Star Capital's multi-class equity structure, described below. However, sponsor fees and waterfalls apply to virtually any equity structure, including the dual-tranche structure described in the previous chapter. I'll conclude by introducing promote crystallization, a unique and rarely used tool that may prove advantageous for sponsors and investors in certain scenarios.

Multi-Class Equity Structure

A multi-class equity structure includes more than one class of common equity investors, often divided into Class A and Class B members. These classes usually have different investment minimums, different terms, and/or different control rights. We recently introduced multi-class deal structures to entice larger investors to commit $500,000+ in deals to qualify as Class B members in our operating agreement. In turn, Class B investors are given preferential terms, or "major investor status." Our typical terms include a $100,000 minimum investment, an 8% cumulative/compounding preferred return, a 30% promote up to a 15% IRR, and a 50% promote thereafter. However, for Class B members receiving major investor status, the minimum investment is $500,000, the preferred return is 9%, and there is a 30% promote with no additional promote tiers. This enhanced deal structure provides an approximately 1% higher projected IRR (17% net IRR instead of 16%) and superior downside protection through the higher preferred return.

The important point to note about this structure is that Class A and Class B investors are pari passu – Latin for "with an equal step" or "on equal footing." In deal structures, when two members or classes are pari passu it means that they receive their share of distributable cash flow on a prorated basis (with no priority given to either group) based on their capital contribution. Even though Class B investors are owed a higher preferred return, this in no way impacts the returns of Class A investors. The enhanced Class B economics are funded solely out of the GP's share of the deal. Essentially, the sponsor is foregoing a portion of the promote by providing major investors a better deal.

The dual-tranche equity structure discussed in the previous chapter, on the other hand, utilizes a senior/subordinate system to reallocate risk/returns to various investment members. In this structure, Class A (pref equity) is owed a fixed rate of return (typically 9% or 10%), which is paid out before Class B (common equity) receives any distributions. In other words, Class A members are senior to Class B members. This structure provides for a cash flow and value cushion since all the cash flow and sale distributions are first owed to the Class A members. In exchange for being subordinate to Class A members' preferred distribution and return of capital, Class B members receive all the upside above the fixed rate of return. Moreover, Class B's returns are enhanced, assuming project-level returns exceed the cost of the Class A capital, which is usually 9% or 10%. Because of these higher projected returns, Class B members are willing to accept the greater level of risk that comes with being subordinate to Class A members.

Additionally, since most deals have projected cash flows below the Class A member preferred distribution rate of 9% or 10%, Class B members in a dual-tranche structure see lower cash flow distributions than they otherwise would. However, if the deal works out, the returns upon sale are more substantial. This senior/subordinate structure is very different from the pari passu nature of the multi-class structure described earlier. The complexity of these structures makes it crucial that you fully understand the mechanics of the deal structure you aim to employ and, in particular, pay attention to the way each deal structure allocates risk and rewards.

Sponsor Fees

Fees are a significant source of compensation for sponsors. Sponsors rely on fees to build their business and earn them by acquiring new properties, managing their portfolio, and sometimes by disposing of or refinancing assets. Acquisition fees are usually 1% to 3% of the purchase price of the asset but may sometimes be calculated based on the total capitalization of the project (purchase price + budgeted capital expenditures). The acquisition fee is paid at closing and is factored into the total amount of equity the sponsor needs to raise. Another fee that may be charged at closing is the capital placement fee, which compensates either the sponsor or an intermediary for raising the capital required to close the deal. Capital placement fees usually range from 2% to 5% of the equity amount. However, this type of fee is rarely used compared to an acquisition fee. A loan guarantee fee is another somewhat common upfront deal fee, which compensates the sponsor or a specific person on the sponsor team for guaranteeing the loan. A loan guarantee fee is seen on both recourse and non-recourse loans and ranges from 0.5% to 2% of the loan amount. All of these fees are essentially acquisition fees in that they are all upfront fees.

Along with the upfront fees, asset management fees are collected monthly/quarterly and are usually 1% to 2% of the property's revenue. Make sure to confirm that the deal's asset management fees are in fact based on revenue and not equity, which is a much larger number and thus reduces investor returns. Refinance fees are usually 1% of the loan amount and are paid by the partnership. Disposition fees are paid at sale and are usually 1% of the sale price. Both disposition and refinance fees compensate the sponsor for the effort required to execute a refinance or sale; however, neither is standard and may be indicative of a high fee load.

Investors should consider fees within the context of the entire fee schedule and deal structure to determine whether the deal is competitive or unattractive. This holds true for every aspect of the deal. It's not necessarily fair to assess a deal or deal structure based on just one fee or term. However, a single fee or deal term that is way out of line could be a dealbreaker – not only is it uncompetitive, but it could also indicate that the sponsor is attempting to take advantage of their investors rather than align interests.

Waterfalls

Beyond fees, deals include a profit-sharing structure known as a waterfall or promote structure. The essential foundation of a good waterfall is a preferred return. A preferred return is a minimum return threshold provided to LPs prior to the payment of any performance compensation or promote to the sponsor.

I highly advise against setting up a deal structure without a preferred return and similarly caution investors not to invest in deals without this component. Not having a preferred return is simply uncompetitive and, in most cases, a sign of the sponsor attempting to take advantage of unwitting passive investors.

Furthermore, not all preferred returns are created equal. Aside from the base rate, which is typically 6% to 9%, preferred returns can differ mechanically. Preferred returns can be compounding or non-compounding. Compounding means that shortfalls in preferred return are not simply accrued but are accrued with interest at the preferred return rate. This protects investors in the event of cash flow distributions less than the preferred return. Non-compounding preferred returns, on the other hand, carry no "penalty" for the sponsor if they do not meet the preferred return distributions.

Moreover, preferred returns may incorporate the return of invested capital, meaning passive investors are entitled to their preferred return as well as a 100% return of their original investment prior to any profit-sharing with the sponsor. This type of preferred return provides additional protection to investors since they wouldn't pay any performance compensation until after they've received their original investment back plus a minimum return (preferred return), usually of 8%. I recommend using this preferred return since it's the most favorable for your investors and turns your deal structure into a selling point.

After the preferred return is satisfied, profit-sharing kicks in. Typically, 60% to 80% of profits above the preferred return are paid to passive investors, with the remaining balance paid to the sponsor(s). However, the share of profits given to investors and sponsors may vary depending on other factors. For example, an investment's uniqueness or difficulty of execution can sometimes justify a more favorable profit split for the sponsor. Secondary hurdles can also be implemented to increase the sponsor's profit split as the returns increase for passive investors. These hurdles can be set up according to the investment's internal rate of return (IRR), the standard compounding return calculation methodology accepted in private equity investments.

To put it all together, here is a common Lone Star Capital waterfall structure:

- Acquisition Fee – 2% of purchase price
- Asset Management Fees – 2% of revenue
- Preferred Return – Compounding 8% plus 100% return of original investment
- Profit Split – 70% to investors up to 15% IRR, 50% to investors above 15% IRR

As discussed above, an industry standard or institutional waterfall includes a cumulative and compounding preferred return, which is also subject to a return of capital prior to the sponsor's promote (performance compensation) kicking in. The elegance of this structure is that this priority of distributions remains consistent across cash flow, refinance proceeds, and sale proceeds. However, other structures may adjust the cash flow distribution to allow the sponsor's promote to kick in after the preferred return is met but prior to returning all capital. This is not necessarily fair to investors since the sponsor could earn performance compensation but then underperform or lose capital later without a clawback of their compensation. While clawbacks are more common in hedge fund structures, clawbacks are very rare in real estate partnership structures. In any case, this is not a big deal in today's environment since cash flows are rarely larger than preferred returns.

Consistent with the aforementioned structure, refinance proceeds should first be used to pay any accrued preferred return. If the preferred return is already current or there are excess proceeds after making the preferred return current, the remaining proceeds should be used to pay down investors' capital accounts. An important distinction to make is that although investors receive a return of capital that pays down their capital account, this does not reduce their ownership percentage in the deal. According to the institutional waterfall, investors' ownership can never be diluted. Even if 100% of capital is returned to investors, they would still own the same percentage of the deal and continue to receive distributions split at the waterfall rate. For example, if a deal has a 70/30 split (70% for investors / 30% promote) above an 8% preferred return and 100% of capital has been returned via a refinance, then every dollar of cash flow or sale proceeds from thereon out would be split 70/30.

However, there are some other structures out there that are unfavorable to investors particularly as it relates to refinancing. For example, some structures consider the payback of investor capital through a refinance as a way for the GP to "buy out" the LPs, allowing the sponsor to own a disproportionate share or the whole deal. This effectively treats the LPs like debt or preferred equity in that they don't participate in the full upside of the deal and are subject to being bought out.

For a value-add investment, this waterfall structure is even more unfair because the LPs enter the deal early on when risk is at the highest. Once value is created and the deal is stabilized, investors are bought out through the refinance rather than being able to enjoy the upside and stabilized returns created as a result of their investment. Additionally, there usually is no capital subordination in these structures, which means the LP capital sits in a first-loss position in the capital stack. This means LPs are taking on full equity-like risk and receiving debt-like returns. This waterfall structure is most commonly implemented on deals that have the potential for a full cash-out refinance. These types of deals are the heaviest of lifts, meaning they are much riskier than the average value-add deal.

As mentioned previously, LPs' ownership is not diluted by a refinance in an institutional waterfall structure because changing the debt does not change the ownership percentages on the deal. Furthermore, a true institutional structure requires the refinance to be used to return all capital and meet the preferred return before the sponsor can participate in any refinance proceeds. This makes the most sense since, even though the cash-out refinance may be a result of value creation, this value creation would not have been possible without financing from investors. Moreover, because there is still a possibility of underperformance in the future, paying back investors' capital should be prioritized over paying the sponsor their promote.

This refinance scenario is one of the reasons I do not recommend straying away from institutional, industry-standard deal structures. You don't want your deal structure to be a sticking point that repels investors, nor do you want to stand out negatively from the competition.

Promote Crystallization

One way the institutional waterfall structure falls short is that it incentivizes sponsors to sell assets sooner rather than later because they want to monetize their promote. This means that if a property has appreciated, the sponsor may have a nice cash promote upon sale. Conversely, if they choose to hold the deal instead, they're delaying the time at which they make their big profit as well as risk the investment going down in value later and losing their promote.

However, some investors prefer to own property for a longer period of time (ten-year hold versus three-year hold), which may create tension between sponsor and investor. A solution to this mismatch is a promote crystallization – a provision in a joint venture agreement whereby the sponsor can capitalize on the value created and thus receive their promote before the asset is sold. In lieu of the sponsor selling and receiving their promote in cash, the partnership reallocates ownership percentages in favor of the sponsor to compensate them for value created. This incentive mechanism is most commonly used in development deals where the partnership would like to hold the completed asset long-term for consistent cash flow.

Through a promote crystallization, the sponsor can reap the rewards of the value created through their development efforts prior to a sale by increasing their ownership percentage in the project and thereby enjoying greater cash flows. This partnership feature is called a "crystallization" because the waterfall structure entitling investors to a preferred return is abandoned (frozen) after the crystallization event occurs. In other words, the sponsor and the rest of the investors receive distributions on a pari passu (equal) basis moving forward. To perform a crystallization, the partnership must go through the motions of a hypothetical sale by agreeing upon a sale valuation and closing costs. The hypothetical net sale proceeds are then run through the originally agreed upon waterfall to calculate how much promote would be owed to the sponsor in a hypothetical sale scenario.

Let's use some numbers to make the example clearer. Suppose that the sponsor originally invested $500,000 into the project in a 90/10 split (contributing 10% of the total equity requirement) and would receive a

$500,000 promote in the event of a sale. To crystallize the promote, the partnership would agree to adjust the 90/10 ownership percentage to 80/20, allocating the sponsor an additional 10% to compensate them for their hypothetical promote. After the partnership crystallizes the new ownership percentages at 80/20, all distributions from cash flows, refinance, or future sale shall be split at the 80/20 ownership percentages.

This structure is a great way to motivate a sponsor to stay in a deal after the initial value creation. Investors can also benefit from this structure since their capital will no longer be subject to a sponsor promote following the crystallization. However, the biggest drawback of promote crystallizations is their complexity. It may be incredibly difficult for sponsors and investors to fairly agree on a valuation for the hypothetical sale. Obviously, it's in the sponsor's best interest to argue for a higher valuation while it's in the investor's best interest to negotiate a lower value. An appraisal or even a broker opinion of value (BOV) can be used to determine the value, but both may leave sponsors and investors desiring more clarity/certainty as to the true fair market value.

I personally believe the crystallization should be done at a slight discount to the appraised/BOV value given the certainty and ease of the transaction, especially since it's not an arm's length deal. The operating agreement should also allow for either party to elect to move forward on an outright sale if one is not happy with the proposed value of the crystallization. While my company, Lone Star Capital, has never employed a promote crystallization, we are working on a strategy that entails developing the multifamily property and crystallizing the promote upon refinancing out of the construction loan. This will allow us to hold the property long-term in a win-win structure with our investors and fairly use the appraisal from the refinance as the crystallization value. An additional benefit of crystallizing in conjunction with a refinance is that it allows you to utilize some or all of the cash-out refinance proceeds to pay a portion of the promote out via cash, with the rest paid in equity.

This strategy works very well with our existing multifamily value-add strategy since it allows us to scale our portfolio with every developed asset rather than immediately sell off the newly constructed property. Keeping a newly built asset in our portfolio is highly attractive because it doesn't have any deferred maintenance and is less likely to have unexpected repairs come up, making it ideal for a longer-term hold.

EQUITY INVESTORS

The main types of equity investors in commercial real estate are retail, co-GP, and joint venture/institutional. I also discuss 1031 exchange investors, a smaller subset of investors that take advantage of the 1031 exchange tax break, which is one of the most powerful tools for investors and an attractive source of capital for sponsors. Below I give you an overview of each of these investors, the role they play in an equity structure, and their goals/preferences when it comes to a deal's profile, structure, and terms. As you read this chapter, keep in mind that some investors fit into multiple categories or may switch between them.

Retail Investors

Retail investors, also known as high-net-worth individuals (HNWI), are the investors that most commonly make up real estate syndications. As you probably already know, a syndication is a deal funded by capital from various investors who usually contribute somewhere between $50K and $250K each. Retail investors usually are not investors by training or profession, but rather are more often high-paid professionals in other fields. These investors are characterized by a smaller check size, which grants them little to no control over a deal's terms or major decisions. Because of this, as well as the more extensive investor relations associated with retail syndications, sponsors earn higher fees and have overall more favorable structures when working with retail investors compared to joint venture equity-style partners.

There are two other very important points to note about retail investors and the syndication deal structure. The first is that retail investors generally have a lower return hurdle than their joint venture/institutional investor counterparts. This is because a private equity firm or opportunity fund investing in a value-add multifamily deal is going to have to justify not only paying your promote but taking their own fees and promote before giving their fund investors the net economics. This "double promote" situation forces investment funds to demand lower fees and higher return hurdles. The second point is that a sponsor substantially reduces their investor concentration risk when structuring a deal as a syndication since the partnership is between the sponsor and many investors rather than one large investor.

I will discuss the dynamics of having one large investor in greater detail later, but for now you should recognize the risks and potential destruction of momentum associated with pursuing and locking in a single-check investor. If that single investor decides to pull out of the deal, it could wreak havoc on your whole process and force you into scramble mode. Similarly, a joint venture investor might try to renegotiate the terms of the deal at the last minute, leaving you with the difficult choice of accepting the new, likely less favorable terms or again pivoting completely to a new investor or project. This underscores the importance of choosing investors carefully, taking into consideration the level of trust in your relationship as well as the investor's reputation in the real estate space.

Even when your total capital raise is diversified among dozens of investors in a retail syndication, you should still do your best to choose reliable investors. Since there are so many, and they aren't making a huge multi-million-dollar decision, retail investors are more capricious and will commit and back out of a deal more frequently. For both retail investors and large joint venture partners, it's important to build many strong relationships so as to avoid being overly reliant upon one individual or group.

Co-General Partners

The next subset of investors is co-general partners or Co-GPs. Co-GP is used to describe investors/partners in a unique partnership structure. The Co-GP structure typically consists of a manager/operator partner and one or more capital partners. The responsibility of the capital partner is to provide LP equity, usually by raising it from retail investors. Additionally, the capital partner co-GP may or may not invest in the GP equity or LP equity in the process of raising LP equity for the deal (some deals don't differentiate between GP and LP equity, while others do). The compensation for raising capital comes in the form of GP interest and economics such as participation in the acquisition fee, asset management fees, and promote. Depending on the structure and the number of partners, this co-GP method of raising capital can be the costliest since you have to deliver returns to the LP investors as well as give up a portion of your GP compensation to the capital-raising co-GP(s). Co-GPs typically provide anywhere from $500,000 to $5MM of equity for a given deal.

Co-GPs that raise a minority portion of the equity, $1MM out of $4MM for example, would command less control and a less favorable share of the economics compared to a co-GP bringing in the majority or the whole equity check. In this scenario, a co-GP raising capital can expect to receive somewhere around 30% of the GP promote on a prorated basis. This means that if they raise $1MM out of $4MM, they could expect to receive 7.5% of the GP economics ($1,000,000/$4,000,000 * 30% of GP allocated to raising capital).

In a majority co-GP scenario, the math is a little different. If a co-GP is bringing 51% to 100% of the equity, they're likely going to want 50% of the promote as well as their fair share of the fees. The promote split is less negotiable, but if you found the deal off-market, you can make the argument that you're entitled to a larger portion of the acquisition fee. Similarly, if you are going to be handling the vast majority of asset management responsibilities as the operating partner, then your company should be able to take home the bulk of the asset management fees.

Giving away 50% of your GP economics is the most expensive way to get a deal done but may very well be worth it if you otherwise wouldn't have a chance at closing the deal at all. Additionally, co-GPs can provide a ton of value, especially to less experienced sponsors. Their support and involvement in the deal can enable you to grow quickly and scale your portfolio by removing major obstacles such as a lack of capital, thereby increasing your ability to put deals under contract and qualify for loans.

Whether a co-GP is coming in for a minority equity contribution or the whole check, there are important value-adds that a co-GP can provide, such as funding pursuit costs, cosigning the loan, and backing the deal with their powerful reputation/experience to help with the overall capital raise. Pursuit costs include travel, due diligence, earnest money deposit, lender deposit, and third-party reports. These out-of-pocket costs can run into the hundreds of thousands and can be a sticking point for newer sponsors trying to put a deal under contract. A more experienced and financially strong partner can come in as a co-GP and help with these upfront costs.

Similarly, a strong co-GP can cosign the loan with you in order to satisfy the lender's experience, net worth, and liquidity requirements, all of which can hold emerging sponsors back from taking on larger properties. This is because lenders typically require the borrower to have a net worth equal to the loan balance, which is obviously not easy to do when starting out if you are seeking $10MM+ loans. Lastly, associating your company and your deal with a better-known co-sponsor benefits your reputation. This cachet can boost your own capital-raising efforts for the co-GP deal as well as deals outside of the co-GP.

Similar to joint venture equity, which we will go into shortly, majority co-GP partners typically require certain controls in the partnership such as major decision rights. This can potentially add a layer of complexity since your investors have to be comfortable with your co-GP partner having control over the deal in some respect. While not a cure-all, it's very helpful to have your major co-GP partner put real skin in the game by way of cash investment. Regardless of whether or not they're cosigning on the loan, real skin in the game from any party can only be achieved via a true out-of-pocket cash investment. This can help mitigate some of the risks of the partnership and better align interests.

I highly recommend that you require any potential controlling co-GP to have some form of skin in the game. Ideally, the investment would come from the principal(s) of the co-GP company or from the company itself. It can come by way of deferring any fees associated with the deal, but really the number one form of skin in the game is cash invested out of pocket by principles on the same terms as yourself and other investors. Sometimes partners will want to invest in the deal but ask for their investment to be structured a certain way, usually with greater protections. This doesn't have to be a deal-killer, but it isn't the same as true skin in the game.

Co-GPs where one or more partners are responsible for raising capital can be handled in various ways. Firstly, you have to determine whether the co-GP is going to provide the capital via a single entity and investment or whether they're going to allow their investors to invest directly into the deal's single purpose vehicle. Either is perfectly acceptable. If the latter option is chosen, the next step is to determine how communication with said investors will be handled. Some co-GPs are comfortable with the lead sponsor/operating partner communicating directly with their investors while others prefer to maintain a firewall of communication so the co-GP can better control the narrative and "stay in front of" their investors.

From the operating sponsor's perspective, it's certainly better to have one point of contact for a large group of investors as well as to have the investment coming in by way of a single check. For example, Lone Star Capital partners with a family office that has brought many of its family members and close friends into our deals, but for the most part, we have maintained a single point of contact. As a result, our communication efforts do not need to be duplicated nor do we constantly hear from multiple investors about how they think things should be run or whether or not we should sell.

An important point to note about this relationship is the sensitivity of handing over one's investors to another sponsorship group. Often, investors don't know who is who nor are they aware of how compensation is allocated according to the investor's entrance into the deal (i.e. whether they're coming in through a co-GP or directly through the sponsor). For this reason, investors may attempt to benignly become a direct investor of the lead sponsor in a future deal and inadvertently cut out the co-GP that introduced them to said sponsor. Sponsors and capital raisers must remain vigilant for situations like this since this is unfair to a capital raiser/co-GP and can strain relationships. My team has been on both sides of this equation and has always made sure to fairly compensate a capital raiser if one of their investors approaches us directly. To ensure everything stays clean and organized, we assign a tag to investors coming from their respective co-GP in our investor portal so we know exactly to whom we can attribute an investor.

Finally, I'd like to reiterate that Co-GP partnerships are often extremely beneficial to all parties involved. Whether you are fulfilling the responsibility of raising capital or are the lead GP putting the deal together, there is much to be gained from sharing the responsibilities and the rewards. This is especially true for those who are newer in the business and are looking to grow their reputation and hands-on experience. Raising capital in a co-GP format for a more experienced operator is a great way to begin building your track record while learning from a company that may be one or several steps ahead.

Joint Venture Partners

The next type of capital partner is a joint venture (JV) equity partner. Groups that partner in this way can range from ultra-high net worth individuals (UHNWI) to family offices, opportunity funds, and more. Typically, JV equity partners are investing $5MM to $20MM per deal, but there are some that write checks above and below this range, which can be valuable to you depending on your strategy and deal size. It's important to understand each individual partner's investment requirements since there is often less flexibility and more nuance in their capital deployment strategy. Whereas a retail investor may be open to many different kinds of opportunities, certain private equity funds may have a tighter "box" in which they invest. For example, many investment firms that fall under this category require that leverage not exceed 70% or that the property be built within the last 30 years.

Similarly, JV partners are usually more selective when it comes to the markets in which they invest, and frankly, most of them prefer to stay in larger growth markets. Some strong examples of markets like these today are Phoenix, Denver, Dallas, Atlanta, Charlotte, and Tampa. You should keep this in mind when determining which capital partners would be the right fit for your investment strategy. For example, if you prefer to focus on secondary/tertiary markets, you would need to seek out the smaller pool of capital that is open to those markets, focusing your capital-raising efforts on retail investors and co-GP partners, who are usually more amenable to smaller markets.

While perceived as more institutional and potentially "ruthless", joint venture partners are still looking to partner with operators they know, like, and trust. This is no different than retail investors, but with the added difficulty of ensuring that the numbers stack up to their rigorous requirements.

It's better to focus on deals with $15MM+ in total capitalization since a more institutional-sized asset will attract a broader range of JV equity partners. The best way to learn what each individual or group is looking for is by asking them in plain terms and taking thorough notes. Consistently doing so will enable you to build a robust understanding and database of equity partners. This knowledge will be essential when deciding who to share certain types of deals with. Additionally, you should be continuously pitching new deals to JV equity partners. This is the best way for both sides to get to know each other by better understanding each other's strategy and underwriting. Moreover, you might be surprised by which deal gets an investor excited so you never know what the feedback will be.

With that being said, most JV equity partners are extremely selective because they have a variety of sponsors vying for their capital and must carefully invest on behalf of their fund investors. As mentioned earlier, private equity firms and opportunity funds have to pay the sponsor's promote and charge their own fees/promote before earning a profit for their investors. This "double promote" situation forces JV equity partners to seek higher returns in order to provide attractive net of fee returns to its fund investors.

I will go into further detail about JV equity structures, but for now the main distinction to understand is that JV equity partners are the limited partner in the structure and you, the sponsor/operator, are the GP. The LP doesn't participate in the GP economics but still has major decision rights such as the decision to refinance, sell, and approval of major capital expenditures. In this deal structure, the LP and GP have separate classes of ownership and separate capital accounts. This means that the GP is not investing in the deal as an LP but is instead investing in GP equity. GP and LP equity are essentially the same thing (both a form of common equity), but the deal structure merges the sponsor's invested equity economics and it's promote economics into the same ownership class. The fees (typically acquisition fees and asset management fees) are paid by the deal pro rata based on capital contribution. Typically, JV equity partners contribute 90% of the required equity for the transaction and therefore pay 90% of the deal fees.

Although the equity not contributed by the JV equity partner is called GP equity, it's not always required for this equity to come directly from the GP's pocketbook. Most JV partners understand that a GP usually doesn't have millions of dollars ready to contribute to every deal and are therefore comfortable with the GP raising their GP equity from private investors. This puts many sponsors at ease since they often wrongly assume they must bring $1MM+ to the table themselves in order to partner with a joint venture equity partner. However, it's worthwhile to have a conversation with a potential capital partner about their GP equity requirements before spending too much time on due diligence, since this can be a gating issue.

I've found that there are four stances a JV equity partner usually takes in regard to GP equity. First, the equity partner requires the GP to contribute 5 to 10% of the equity and the equity must come from the GP's balance sheet. Second, the equity partner requires the GP to contribute 5 to 10% of the equity but is comfortable with it coming from the GP's balance sheet and that of their family members. Third, the LP requires 5 to 10% GP equity contribution and doesn't care at all about where the money comes from, meaning the GP is free to syndicate the equity from their network of retail investors. Fourth, the JV equity partner has no GP equity requirement. Knowing what type of requirement your JV equity partner has upfront can save you a lot of trouble and headache.

While many JV equity partners are flexible on GP equity requirements, very few are willing to cosign on the loan with you. So if your internal sponsorship team isn't able to qualify for the loan on their own, you can either seek out a loan guarantor whose principal responsibility in the deal is to sign on the loan, or you can find a co-GP who will bring equity to the table and sign on the loan. A loan cosigner typically charges somewhere between 0.5% to 1.0% of the loan amount as a loan guarantor fee and usually receives 15 to 25% of the GP economics.

In my experience, it's better to find partners who take on a bigger role in the deal and satisfy as many of the responsibilities as possible. Parceling out more roles/responsibilities usually results in giving away more of the deal than you otherwise would. For this reason, it may be unattractive to bring on a JV equity partner and a co-GP partner on the same deal since you'd be giving away so much of the deal's economics and leaving little for yourself.

Let's go back to the JV equity scenario where the sponsor brings in retail investors to satisfy their GP equity requirement. In this case, it's important to note that you don't have to raise the retail investor equity for your GP equity requirement on the same terms as the JV equity. For example, the JV equity may only be paying a 1% acquisition fee and demand a 10% preferred return. However, you can still charge a 2% acquisition fee to the retail investors coming into the deal via the GP equity. Similarly, the GP equity investors can be offered an 8% pref, earning the sponsor a greater promote on that portion of the equity.

It's common for there to be confusion as to how varying preferred returns in the same deal work. If one class of investor receives an 8% preferred return and another a 10% preferred return, there is no subordination between the two classes of members. In other words, the investors from the 8% and 10%

pref class are pari passu, receiving their share of distributable cash flow pro rata based on their capital contribution.

For example, let's say there are two investors each investing $1MM where one investor receives an 8% preferred return and the other receives a 10% preferred return. If there is $180,000 of distributable cash flow for a given year, each investor would receive $90,000 but in different ways. The investor with an 8% preferred return would have their pref ($80,000) satisfied, with the remaining $10,000 used to either pay down the investor's $1,000,0000 capital account down to $990,000 or to give a cash flow promote depending on the deal structure. The 10% pref investor would equally receive $90,000 but would not see their preferred return ($100,000) satisfied and would accrue the outstanding $10,000 to the following period. Also, depending on the deal structure, this shortfall in the 10% pref would compound, earning interest at the 10% preferred return rate until paid.

 As you can see, the investors have different outcomes associated with the same $90,000 distribution, but neither is paid first. In sum, GP equity and LP equity share in the cash flow on an equal basis (proportionate to their capital input) in a JV equity partnership. The pari passu nature of JV deals distinguishes it from the dual-tranche equity structure, which is characterized by its senior-subordinate hierarchy of preferred and common equity investors.

A major difference between the partnership structure of most syndications and that of more institutional joint ventures is the fact that the preferred return is an IRR hurdle, rather than simply a cash flow based pref. This means the sponsor's promote is subordinate to a 100% return of capital as well as a cumulative and compounding preferred return. While most people are familiar with the preferred return concept, an IRR hurdle is foreign to them. Yet, it's undoubtedly important for sponsors and investors to understand because it affects the sponsor's cash flow based promote and investors' downside protection. In a syndication, if the preferred return of let's say 8% is paid in a given monthly or quarterly distribution and there is surplus cash flow, that surplus cash flow will be split with the sponsor and investors according to the promote rate (often 70% to investors and 30% to the sponsor). This is known as a cash flow promote because the sponsor receives compensation from the excess cash flow generated by the investment.

Implementing an IRR hurdle makes it almost impossible for the sponsor to earn a cash flow promote. This is because the cash flows are first paid to satisfy any outstanding preferred return, and if there is any surplus, all of it goes towards returning the investors' originally invested capital. For example, if 10% cash flow is generated, the first 8% would go towards satisfying the preferred return and the subsequent 2% would be distributed to reduce the investor's capital account down to 98% of their original investment. In a shortfall scenario, any unpaid preferred return would accumulate and compound to the following period. For example, if only 6% is available to be distributed, all of it would go towards the preferred return payment, and the 2% shortfall on the preferred return (assuming an 8% pref) would be added to the investors' capital account. In effect, this would increase the investors' investment to 102% of their original capital input. Furthermore, the following period's preferred return is calculated based on the new, 102% higher capital account, thereby compounding the preferred return. This means that the investors are earning the 8% preferred return rate on the 2% that was unpaid from the previous distribution period.

In our syndications at Lone Star Capital, we choose to employ an IRR hurdle even if our investors don't recognize or appreciate the full benefits of it. In fact, many investors are unfamiliar with IRR hurdles and their benefits (except, of course, our institutional partners, who wouldn't do a deal any other way). We choose to employ an IRR hurdle because it aligns interests well and maximizes the cash flow we can deliver to investors. I recommend this structure to sponsors since it's relatively straightforward to explain and makes your deal stand out positively to investors.

1031 Exchange Investors

1031 exchange investors include any retail, co-GP and JV investors that have 1031 exchange funds for which they seek a passive investment opportunity. A 1031 exchange is a major tax benefit associated with real estate ownership that allows the deferral of capital gains taxes by exchanging an asset for a like-kind property upon sale rather than receiving all the sale proceeds in taxable cash. Combining a 1031 exchange with a sponsored investment allows a 1031 exchange investor to essentially become an LP in a professionally managed investment vehicle. The investor performing the 1031 exchange into the venture can also 1031 exchange out their interest upon sale because their interest in the venture is via a tenancy-in-common (TIC). The TIC allows the investor to exchange their interest upon sale irrespective of the actions of the other members in the venture or the manager. This is advantageous since typically LPs in a real estate investment are unable to 1031 exchange their individual ownership interest upon sale and must rely on a deal-level 1031 exchange if they wish to defer capital gains taxes upon sale. This is because limited partners technically do not own real estate. Instead, they own a partnership interest in a real estate venture, which is ineligible for a 1031 exchange since 1031 exchanges must be like-kind exchanges of real property.

To elaborate, the TIC structure enables the 1031 investor to take direct title to the property, thereby fulfilling one of the key requirements of a legitimate 1031 exchange. A complication of the TIC structure within a management partnership is that the "tenants" in common have joint and several ownerships of the property with equal control. However, in a syndication/joint venture, the sponsor is supposed to have decision-making control (this is important to the lender as well since they're lending based on the sponsor's control and ability to oversee the success of the deal). Typical joint venture economics and control rights can be outlined through a side-letter or through other means in order to make the 1031 fit into a traditional syndication/joint venture structure.

Not all sponsors offer their investors the opportunity to 1031 exchange, so it's a great way to stand out, if your team is willing to develop the expertise and put in the extra effort to structure deals this way. To learn more about 1031 exchanges in syndications, watch my recent webinar on the topic here[2].

Our team has experience structuring 1031 exchanges in our investments both with agency lenders, bridge debt, and banks. The greatest source of complexity comes from the lender requirements when it comes to the TIC structure, especially when lending from Fannie Mae and Freddie Mac. Because the 1031 TIC investor is a direct owner of the property, they're technically a borrower in the eyes of the lender and therefore must be underwritten. Being underwritten by a lender requires a credit check, background check, disclosure of personal financial statements, schedule of real estate owned, and business resume. This doesn't mean the 1031 investor has to be a guarantor on the loan, but sometimes lenders ask for limited guarantees. We handle this entire process for our 1031 exchange investors as well as form and manage the single purpose entity (the vehicle holding title on behalf of the 1031 investor, as required by the lender).

---

[2] See the 1031 Exchange Webinar on YouTube here:
https://bit.ly/1031exchangewebinar

RETURN EXPECTATIONS

Let's talk about return expectations and deal/risk profiles across the various investor types. It's important to know your audience and to find the right type of investor to fit the strategy or deal profile you're pursuing. For example, retail investors are generally more concerned about consistent cash-on-cash returns, whereas certain types of institutional investors may be perfectly happy investing in a deal that doesn't produce any cash flow for the first year or two, assuming there will eventually be a large payout via a refinance or a sale. Similarly, some institutional investors set a very high bar for their target returns (often due to the double promote nature of their fund structure as discussed before) and therefore will rule out great opportunities that simply are not risky enough and, accordingly, don't project high enough returns. This means that a perfectly good deal with strong risk-adjusted returns could be passed up because the investor is looking to take on more risk in pursuit of higher returns, even if the deal may be at a worse risk-adjusted return. On the other hand, some institutional investors prefer to take less risk and limit themselves to lower debt leverage and thus will target appropriately lower returns for the types of deals they're comfortable investing in.

Furthermore, some investors evaluate investments based on IRR while others focus on cash-on-cash returns. Thus, as a sponsor, evaluating a deal from a return metric perspective is critical to determining how to present your deals to a prospective investor and align interests. Starting with the most important metric, IRR (internal rate of return) is the total return calculation, which factors in the compounding time value of money. For a given deal, you can observe the projected unlevered IRR (the cash flows and sale profits assuming no debt), gross IRR (the IRR before the sponsor is paid fees and promote), and the net IRR (the IRR that investors are projected to receive after paying all fees and promote). We tend to focus on net IRR since most investors only care about how much money they're projected to make. If a property is newer, well located, and provides steady cash flow, the net IRR may only need to be about 13%. Conversely, if an investment opportunity is 50 years old, located in a class C area, and is 50% vacant, then the projected net IRR may need to be 18%+ to attract investors.

In between 13% and 18%, there are many factors that go into determining the appropriate IRR hurdle. For example, in my opinion, the largest source of risk for a real estate investment is the debt. If the exact same deal is purchased with a bridge loan instead of a lower-risk permanent loan, the IRR hurdle should be anywhere from 2% to 4% higher because of the added leverage/risk. Some may feel this is an expensive premium to demand for an investment funded by a bridge loan, but it really is the bare minimum, given that the bridge loan's added leverage should magnify projected returns, thereby closing the IRR premium gap on its own. Selecting the appropriate IRR hurdle is a key part of every investment strategy, whereas many of the metrics discussed ahead might be more or less important depending on the deal profile.

The second metric we focus on is average cash-on-cash returns throughout the hold period. We typically seek a minimum 5% average cash-on-cash return. This metric may need to be pushed up or down depending on the quality of the asset, its location, and the business plan. For example, a longer-term hold should produce a higher average cash-on-cash return since there is more time to develop the property and build up the cash flow. Another consideration for cash flow is interest-only debt versus amortization. Amortized debt service pays both the principal and interest while following a typical payoff schedule of 30 years. It's valuable to evaluate amortized cash flow in the event interest-only payments expire.

Another factor contributing to risk and return premiums for cash flow are loan assumption deals. A loan assumption contributes to a higher risk profile since a greater portion of the returns are reliant upon a capital event in the future, rather than more certain, consistent, and nearer-term cash flows. Thus, if a property is acquired subject to its existing loan with weak cash flows, we will typically demand a 300-basis point IRR premium. Investors love cash flow and need an enticing reason (higher IRR) to invest in a deal with weak cash flows.

The final but arguably most important metric is yield on cost (YOC) – more precisely, un-trended stabilized yield on cost. YOC is calculated by dividing the stabilized net operating income by the sum of the purchase price and capital expenditures (stab NOI / (price + CapEx)). It's the purest form of valuation since it cannot be manipulated by growth factors, financing, or exit cap rate assumptions. Because of this, sophisticated investors love a true yield on cost calculation as it allows them to cut through the noise and see an investment's true value. We generally look for deals with a minimum 5% YOC but can demand as high as 7% depending on the market and risk profile of the deal. These target metrics often change based on market conditions and financing costs.

Perhaps the most important corollary to yield on cost is the spread between the projected yield on cost and market cap rates (or the exit cap rate) in the model. This spread indicates the true value creation driven by the business plan since the goal of any investment is to create a stream of cash flow at a cost basis that is less than what the market is willing to pay for that stream of cash flow. For a lower-risk investment and a quality market, the minimum spread between YOC and our exit cap rate is 25 basis points. A deal with a YOC equal to the exit cap rate can still project decent returns but must rely on strong rent growth in a top market.

These sorts of nuances are important to grasp if you want to avoid setting yourself up for failure or finding yourself confused when an investor doesn't take interest in your seemingly good deal. What constitutes a "good" deal is subjective and means different things to different investors. However, if you master these metrics and fully understand their implications, you'll be more equipped to find investors that match your deal profile.

Additionally, you must understand how risk factors into investors' decisions. The concept of risk-adjusted returns is foundational in the business of investing. It's commonly assumed that risk and reward are linked in a positively correlated relationship. However, this notion is misleading since higher returns are not guaranteed by more risk. More accurately, projected returns, not necessarily actual returns, increase with greater risk.

For example, in order to entice investors to take even greater risk than a 15% return opportunity, the alternative (higher risk) opportunity must present potential returns in excess of 15%. However, simply having returns greater than 15% may not be enough. Risk is impossible to quantify but hypothetically, an investor would not choose a deal with twice the amount of risk in order to pursue 16% returns instead of 15%. This is where the concept of risk-adjusted returns comes into play. The number itself is insufficient to justify the strength and quality of an investment; the projected returns must be favorable in the context of the deal's risk.

Risk-adjusted returns are of paramount importance when determining the deal profile for your first deal. If you have no track record and are looking to acquire your first investment property, I highly recommend you buy a stabilized asset with long-term financing that produces strong cash flow from day one. While this may not be the investment strategy of choice for you and the many operators who prefer more value-add opportunities, the deal type described above is typically a better fit for your first deal for a few reasons. First, a cash-flowing investment presents less execution risk, especially if it's financed with long-term debt since this takes maturity risk largely out of the equation. Secondly, by producing and distributing cash flow on a monthly or quarterly basis to your investors from day one, you will more quickly build up your "track record." I place track record in quotes because making a few monthly distributions in the initial period of ownership is far from the track record of multiple round trips (acquisition to sale) that's desired by investors. However, it's still a good start in terms of growing your reputation, and at least initially, will validate your business model and indicate a path to success.

By providing strong distributions even in just the first few months of ownership, you will have a decent portion of your first-time investors ready to commit more capital to your next investment opportunity. Conversely, if your first deal is a deep value-add opportunity that produces no cash flow in the first six months or year, you'll find it difficult to convince your investors to partner with you on subsequent deals until you've shown them some distributions in your first acquisition. Evidently, this can slow down your progress in terms of jumping into new opportunities and building your track record.

RAISING RETAIL EQUITY

Now that you've acquainted yourself with the various types of investors and deal structures, let's take a deeper dive into the various capital-raising strategies that will help you maximize your success. In this chapter, I'll discuss strategies for raising retail equity, both directly from retail investors and indirectly from co-GPs. As discussed previously, retail investors are high net worth individuals (HNWI) who are typically busy professionals that are not focused on real estate investing full-time. Many are doctors, lawyers, or tech professionals and are usually looking for ways to diversify from the stock market and/or generate better cash flow with their investment portfolio. The starting point for many sponsors looking to raise retail capital is in their own friends and family network.

Regardless of the strength or size of your friends and family network, it's always best to start there since there is a built-in element of trust, unlike in a new relationship. However, starting out, your friends and family are likely unaware of your interest in capital raising for real estate syndication investments, and may even underestimate your knowledge and skills in the area. This is why building a thought leadership platform is such an important first step to developing your investor funnel. A thought leadership platform is any medium that allows you to share your message, grow your reach, and build trust. Effective examples are podcasts, YouTube channels, social media, blogs, newsletters, or in-person meet ups.

By consistently producing content and putting yourself in front of your friends and family, as well as other potential investors joining your audience, you will build your reputation as a trusted expert, which will make raising capital a whole lot easier. There are two principal factors that influence your ability to raise retail capital – the size of your potential investor universe and the degree to which that universe likes and trusts you. A hundred loyal investors can be infinitely more powerful and profitable than a lukewarm base of 2,000, but it's nevertheless important to continuously work on growing your audience.

When first starting out, sponsors may find it daunting to go out and meet potential investors outside of their friends and family network. Some effective ways to do this include staying consistent with your thought leadership efforts, being a guest on other people's thought leadership platforms (i.e. podcasts and videos), networking and/or speaking at conferences, contributing to online forums/groups, and making connections with individuals in the online real estate space. By being a guest on someone's podcast, you are exposing yourself and your message to that person's audience, which increases your reach and credibility. Similarly, you can be a guest speaker at an online or in-person meet up or conference and reap the same benefits. It's incredibly important to make the most of these guest appearances by enticing your new audience to join your tribe (follow you on social media and/or join your email list). Arguably the best thing you can do is to get people to sign up for your email list since having someone's email is a far better way to ensure the delivery of your future communications than "friending" on social media. The best way to accomplish this is by hosting a compelling giveaway that entices individuals to drop their name and email on your website or landing page in exchange for valuable information. Examples of attractive giveaway materials are a research whitepaper, guide, e-book, spreadsheet, or video. Almost anything can be turned into a compelling giveaway as long as it's something that resonates with your target audience and adds value to them. By far, my most successful giveaway has been my multifamily underwriting model. Over the years, many people have asked me why I don't sell my model for hundreds of dollars. My response is that by giving it away for free, I've been able to gain thousands of subscribers on my email list. Many of these people have subsequently become loyal followers and/or investors because of the valuable content I provide in my monthly email newsletters and via my other thought leadership.

To maximize your benefit at conferences, I recommend socializing with a wide variety of people but, most importantly, dedicating extra time to those who you actually connect with and can see yourself working with. There is very little value in running around and handing your business card to everyone without building rapport or having meaningful conversations. Instead, you should proactively seek out the investors or partners you would like to meet and collect their business cards. As soon as the conference is over, email each investor/partner a nice, personal follow-up with context from your conversation and add them to your email list. This is great advice but surprisingly, not many people take it. Putting in a little extra effort to send a kind email will go a long way in terms of creating and maintaining investor relations.

As mentioned before, another place to grow your network is via online groups and forums. BiggerPockets is the largest real estate forum and it's full of potential investors. Although I personally haven't relied on BiggerPockets, I know several large sponsors who attribute a tremendous amount of their capital-raising success to being active on BiggerPockets. Facebook groups are another great way to connect with real estate investors as well. You should join popular real estate groups with active and credible members, as well as consider starting your own Facebook group where you can assume authority. Regardless of what platform you're on, being active is the key. You should consistently respond to people's questions and threads as well as start your own conversations. This is no small commitment, and you can't expect to see results in 30 days, but within a year your presence and credibility in the real estate space will grow. Regardless of the type of thought leadership you choose, being consistent over a long period of time is the only way to achieve success.

The strategies mentioned above are terrific for top-of-funnel thought leadership, meaning they catch the attention of potential investors and partners. But, that is only the start of your funnel. You must find ways to create even more value for prospects who move past the top of your funnel and are in the middle of your funnel. As a starting point, sending out a weekly, biweekly, or monthly newsletter consistently is a great way to stay top of mind for your valuable, potential investors. I do not recommend a quarterly newsletter because it's too infrequent and thus allows prospects to forget about you. You'd rather have people on your email list anticipating your emails than forgetting that they'll arrive at all. On the other hand, you want to be careful about burning out your email list by sending too many emails.

Two powerful strategies to avoid burning out your email list are to ensure you're delivering quality content and to segment your email list so you're sending emails to subsets of your audience according to their interests. For example, some of your potential investors may be interested in receiving investment offerings but are not interested in reading your monthly newsletter. Giving your audience the option to unsubscribe from one but not the other is a great way to keep your engagement high and not burn out your audience.

Another way to build further trust and offer more value in the middle of your funnel is through investor introductory phone calls, which give you the opportunity to share more information about your business and investment strategy as well as answer any questions. These phone calls could even be a great place to source ideas for new thought leadership content.

One of my favorite and most influential forms of middle funnel thought leadership is a book (just like this one). A book is versatile in that it can create top-of-funnel engagement, but it's generally more middle-funnel since someone usually needs to be familiar with you and your message prior to investing time and money into reading your book. Another tremendous benefit of publishing a book is the credibility that comes with it. Having a published book can open many doors, such as invitations to be a guest speaker at events and podcasts related to your book topic. The credibility associated with being a published author can make it easier to land meetings with potential investors and partners. The other amazing thing about writing a book is that it's rare. While some sponsors and investors may have the domain expertise necessary to write a book, very few have the drive. Writing a book shows you're both knowledgeable and dedicated, which are major trust-building factors differentiating you from the crowd.

As potential investors move further down your funnel, they will grow more interested not only in your content but in your business. It's crucial to have your company information organized and put together professionally so that you're ready when potential investors reach out and request more information. You should have the following materials prepared: a company presentation, track record, case studies, sample reporting, testimonials/references, and a sample investment offering. Furthermore, all these key pieces of information should be organized together in an easily accessible folder for investors. Take a look at Lone Star Capital's Company Data Room for an example of these materials put together here[3].

Your company presentation should include your company's backstory, team information, strategy, track record, case studies, and testimonials. Because your track record is so important to investors, it's worth having a standalone track record document outside of your company presentation. Putting your track record together in Excel makes it easier to update and export to PDF. You should be updating it frequently with data on your new acquisitions and successful exits. It's not enough to have a great team, strategy, and track record. If the information is not organized and presented professionally to potential investors, they may pass on you for another sponsor.

At the bottom of the funnel are your investment opportunities. Some of your prospective investors may need to hang out in your middle funnel for a while to build trust before moving further and investing in one of your deals. Other investors may be

---

3 See LSC Company Data Room here:
https://bit.ly/lscdataroom

willing to move straight to the bottom and invest right away. The important point is to have your thought leadership infrastructure built out to properly nurture your audience and prevent potential investors from slipping through the cracks due to inconsistency or lack of a robust marketing system.

Your investment offerings should provide a compelling value proposition in line with the education you provide in your thought leadership. For example, if your thought leadership educates investors on self-storage development, then your investment offerings should stick to that asset class and strategy. Investors like to see focus and consistency, which is why it's crucial to carefully pick an investment strategy and thought leadership strategy and stick to them.

After launching an offering to your investor/partner base, you may want to consider hosting a live webinar to present the deal and secure commitments. If you're a sponsor partnering with co-GPs to help them raise capital, then you must ensure the co-GPs have all the materials and information necessary to be successful with their respective capital raises for the investment. With multiple co-GPs involved, raising capital for a deal can become logistically complicated since investors across various partners are committing and funding on a first come, first served basis. However, co-GPs don't want to put in the effort to be a partner on a deal only to be crowded out by other investor capital. The solution is to reserve a portion of the total equity to each co-GP so that they are essentially guaranteed a minimum amount of equity for the deal.

For example, if a deal requires a total of $5,000,000 in equity, a co-GP partner can be allocated $2,000,000 and any capital over $2,000,000 will be put on a waitlist. Conversely, if the partner being allocated $2,000,000 only brings in $1,000,000 then that creates a gap that must be filled. This is a delicate balance of giving co-GP partners time to raise capital, but not too much time since coming up short at the last minute can cause closing delays. The best thing to do is to set a funding deadline two weeks to a month before the target closing date. If a partner has not met their reserved amount by the funding deadline, then it's the sponsor's responsibility to find capital to close the gap.

Speaking of co-GP partners, as discussed previously, co-GP capital can be a great source of equity, especially when starting out since partners may be more established, have more experience, and have access to more retail capital. You can meet co-GP partners in many of the same ways as regular retail investors, such as through thought leadership, conferences, and social media. It's important to reach out to potential co-GP partners as early in the deal as possible so they have ample time to do due diligence on the sponsor and the deal as well as raise equity from their investors.

When reaching out to co-GP partners, having an organized data room goes a long way. A deal data room should have an investment presentation/memo, property financials, and your underwriting model. This gives potential partners and investors a strong initial understanding of the deal and helps them decide whether to take a deeper dive or not. Additionally, a deal data room includes debt information (i.e. a quote matrix or term sheet), insurance diligence, a cost segregation estimate, general market research such as a CoStar report, and property tax information. Finally, if a deal is at the syndication stage, the deal data room can include the syndication offering documents, such as the private placement memorandum (PPM), subscription agreement (SA), operating/partnership agreements, and wiring instructions. In addition to the deal data room, co-GP partners may benefit from access to your company data room as well, particularly if it's a new relationship and they need to perform sponsor due diligence.

RAISING JOINT VENTURE EQUITY

Many of the tips and strategies discussed regarding retail investors and co-GP partners surprisingly apply to joint venture/institutional equity partners. Some people hold the misconception that because institutional investors are professional and more sophisticated, marketing doesn't work on them. In reality, strong marketing, along with presenting yourself and your company professionally, works on everyone. Furthermore, as the world of crowdfunding and syndications continues to grow, institutional investors such as private equity firms and family offices are becoming more familiar and accepting of this alternative source of capital. In fact, institutional investors even recognize it as a source of competition since their sponsors can potentially raise retail capital at more attractive terms.

Therefore, putting in the effort to excel at both raising retail and institutional capital can pay dividends and even be synergistic. When a capital partner knows you have other options or sees you oversubscribe a deal before they have time to commit, it creates FOMO (fear of missing out) and increases the seriousness with which they will evaluate your company and deal next time.

First, let's take a step back and discuss how to find and build relationships with institutional capital. At the risk of sounding like a broken record, institutional equity relationships can be built in similar ways to retail and co-GP capital. Another great way I like to keep my eye out for new potential equity partners is through press releases and LinkedIn. Press releases posted by brokerage firms and sponsors selling deals may mention who the debt and equity partners are for the deal.

Once a potential equity partner is identified, you can reach out via cold email. Here is my preferred method of reaching out cold to a new equity partner:

"Hi (insert name),

I run a vertically integrated multifamily investment firm focused on Texas workforce housing. We currently have a deal under contract that fits your criteria and are looking for JV equity. Do you have time this week to discuss further?

Thanks,

Rob Beardsley"

This is an effective way to reach out cold and has a surprisingly high response rate. This is because equity providers are deal junkies just as much as sponsors are and thus are often enticed by a deal under contract. This is key; investors like to perform due diligence deals that are actionable, preferably under contract, and available for them to take a majority equity position. If you don't have a deal under contract at the time, you can say that the deal is already taken but that a conversation would still be helpful to prepare each other for the next deal.

Another straightforward way to get in front of institutional equity is by using an equity broker. Equity brokers work similarly to debt brokers and are responsible for reaching out to potential equity partners on your behalf. Equity brokers have a network of capital relationships and should be able to identify which equity sources are the best fit for you and your deal. At the end of the day, equity brokers cannot do your job for you. Just because they have these built-in relationships doesn't mean their equity sources will automatically invest with you. Equity partners are extremely picky and patient, so it's still imperative to put your best foot forward with your company information and track record, as well as present your deal information in a professional manner as discussed previously.

Additional ways to prepare for institutional capital conversations and stand out are to have a focused strategy and single market expertise, have a well-organized track record with at least one round trip (full cycle deal going from acquisition to sale), and to build out a professional team with vertically integrated operations. Investors want sponsors that bring value and expertise to the table. Your value is perceived to be greater the more focused you are. For example, if you are a multifamily sponsor that only buys 2000s vintage assets in Tampa, institutional capital will find you much more attractive than a sponsor that opportunistically buys any kind of deal across the country. This point is more important the smaller you are. Once you reach a certain size, such as $1B in assets under management (AUM), investors will be more comfortable with you focusing on multiple markets and/or multiple strategies. However, when starting out, tackling multiple markets or strategies can shoot you in the foot.

When choosing a market to focus on, you have the option to focus on larger or smaller markets as well as high-growth or low-growth markets. Institutional investors typically prefer large, high-growth markets, but those markets are where the highest competition and biggest deals lie. As a newer sponsor, it may be too tough to break into a market like this or find deals that underwrite attractive returns. However, many institutional investors rule out smaller markets because they do not like the illiquidity and risk that comes with them. Furthermore, smaller markets typically have smaller deals and lower prices per unit, making it harder to find large enough deals to attract institutional investors. This means if your goal is to partner with larger capital partners, you will have to stick to large, well-known markets.

Some institutional investors will invest in older multifamily properties, but most prefer newer assets that are of institutional quality, typically 1990s and newer. Large investors don't mind paying a bit more per unit or paying a lower cap rate to own an asset that presents fewer potential headaches.

Your track record doesn't necessarily need to be robust for you to begin having institutional capital conversations. However, having at least two to three acquisitions under your belt and preferably one sale goes a long way. Furthermore, being sophisticated and transparent on how your track record is presented means a lot. For example, your track record should have dates, purchase prices or total capitalizations, loan amounts, and IRRs. Another great way to stand out when presenting your track record is to have fleshed out case studies for all your exits (and refinances). Your case studies should include the original due diligence information at acquisition (including your underwriting), a case study write-up, and the communications/reporting provided to investors. To see examples of case studies and a track record, visit Lone Star Capital's Company Data Room[4].

Institutional investors want to invest with a professional team. Everyone on your team should be full-time rather than real estate investors on the side. You should strive towards making you and your company appear as professional as possible. Some easy elements to implement are a professional website, professional email addresses, business cards, and a business address. In a world that is getting more and more casual and where working from home has

---

[4] See LSC Company Data Room here:
https://zhat.ty/lxcdataroom

become acceptable, it's still worth it to come across professional when dealing with high-level investors.

It's not common for multifamily private equity firms to have in-house property management, but institutional investors usually highly value vertical integration, and some even require it to partner with them. This is because sponsors in vertically integrated real estate investment firms tend to be more focused and hands-on. For example, our company, Lone Star Capital, is vertically integrated and our in-house property management company, Radiance Living, only manages our portfolio (we don't do any third-party management). This allows our management team to focus solely on our own assets, making the success of Lone Star's investments priority number one. This means that profit at the Radiance Living level is secondary, which allows the team to be spread over a smaller number of communities. Third-party management companies, on the other hand, have a clear incentive to accumulate as many third-party management agreements per as few employees as possible. Instead, our mission is to empower our employees to think outside of the box and go the extra mile when it comes to the implementation of our business plans and the management of our portfolio. Through vertical integration, we believe we can achieve better employee satisfaction and retention and, in turn, more consistent operations. We also have greater visibility into our operations and thus can avoid being blindsided by a problem only becoming apparent in a monthly or quarterly report later down the line.

The final step when preparing to partner with institutional capital is to ensure you have institutional-grade reporting. While most retail investors don't read monthly financials and skim quarterly reports, institutional investors are extremely meticulous and dive deep into reporting. Because institutional investors rely heavily on monthly financials and quarterly reporting, they demand reports be thorough and on time. If you are using a third-party property management company, make sure they can provide robust monthly financial reports that include profit and loss statements, rent roll, budget versus actual reports, general ledgers, bank statements, and more. If you are running property management in-house, it's highly advised to outsource accounting to a professional accounting firm capable of producing institutional-grade reports.

Beyond just accounting reports, quarterly reports produced by the sponsor are also expected to provide insight into the operations. A sponsor's quarterly report should include an analysis of underwriting versus actual performance, which shows how the property performed relative to the underwriting projections shared with investors prior to acquiring the deal. This tool is extremely transparent and helpful for all parties involved, yet surprisingly not all sponsors implement it – meaning it'll make you stand out.

In addition to an underwriting vs actual comparison, we typically create a budget vs actual table. The difference is instead of using the projected numbers from the acquisition underwriting, the budget vs actual table uses our operational budget, which is put together before the start of every calendar year. Comparing the two metrics reveals interesting insights since we refine our budget every year for each property, yet the acquisition underwriting does not change. Over time we can see how our refined budget compares to the assumptions we made before we purchased the property and how close our updated budget compares to our actual performance. This becomes increasingly helpful the longer you own an investment since projections tend to become less meaningful or less accurate the further out they are made.

Other valuable key metrics to include in quarterly reports are the property's cash position, (i.e. reserve account balance), CapEx budget, and operating capital. For example, if the deal began with $100,000 in an operating reserve, an investor would want to know the balance of that reserve on a quarterly basis. If there was a tough month and the operating reserve had to be utilized, you should prepare an explanation and a plan to replenish the account. Additionally, investors should be aware of any utilization of reserve funds to maintain distribution levels. These are simple account balances to track over time but provide valuable insight into the health of the operations.

Lastly, quarterly reports should include a capital expenditures section that outlines the business plan's progress, how much of the budget has been expended, and the actual cost relative to the budget for each line item. This shows investors if the plan is on budget and on schedule. At the conclusion of all the CapEx, there may be leftover funds. This would be a win for investors since the business plan was completed under budget. The remaining capital could be used to fortify reserves or could be returned to investors. Conversely, if the renovations are over budget, the quarterly report can explain this, which can justify reducing distributions. While bad news is never good, by providing context and a lot of quality information, it can be digested more easily. To round out all the numbers in the quarterly report, it's helpful to add commentary where necessary to provide color. Numbers on their own can be confusing or misunderstood, which is why having a good balance between data, charts, and commentary makes for great quarterly reporting.

After you have prepared your team and materials to build investor relationships, you are now ready to put your best foot forward when pitching deals. In addition to sharing your deal data room with financials, market research, underwriting, memos, and other due diligence, it's important to let investors know the status and timeline of the deal upfront. Investors want to know if the deal has been awarded to you or if it's already under contract as well as what the anticipated closing timeline is. It may also be helpful for them to know your equity-raising process and how much time they have to make a decision or to give you a preliminary indication. Moreover, potential partners need to know what their total check size would be and how much of the equity you are expecting them to raise. Having these important points clearly laid out in an email shows you are organized and respect their time.

If there is initial interest, a capital partner will dive into your underwriting and business plan, especially as it relates to your team's track record and ability to execute said plan. Having a solid underwriting model that is rigorous yet easy to understand is extremely valuable. You can download Lone Star Capital's free underwriting model as an example or for your use here[5]. Along with a good model, you must have defensible projections that can be supported by market data such as rent comparables, the market vacancy rate, market growth projections, expense comparables, and so on. Investors are looking to poke holes in your underwriting, so it's up to you to know your numbers inside and out with full confidence. To learn more about multifamily underwriting, check out my book, The Definitive Guide to Underwriting Multifamily Acquisitions[6].

[5] See the LSC Underwriting Model here: https://bit.ly/lscunderwritingmodel

[6] Purchase The Definitive Guide to Underwriting Multifamily Acquisitions here: https://bit.ly/underwritingbook

CONCLUSION

As you explore and consider implementing the various structures and strategies outlined in this book, never lose sight of your goal to create the optimal deal structure for both you and your investors. To achieve this, you must examine the tools in this book, not in isolation, but as part of a bigger picture. For example, how you structure your debt can and should influence how you structure your equity and vice versa. Moreover, market conditions, deal profile, your company's experience, and your investor relationships should play a role in your strategy and decision-making as you raise and structure your capital stack. All of these factors must be considered carefully – individually and collectively – to design the optimal deal structure.

It's also important to keep in mind that the business of doing deals is everchanging – making it all the more fun. How you anticipate and respond to these changes will determine whether or not you succeed. As a sponsor, you should aim to buy and develop real estate throughout the entire market cycle. This means you'll have to shift structures/strategies as market conditions, deal profiles, and other factors change.

You must be versatile and inventive to survive and thrive in the dynamic real estate business. It'll be incredibly difficult to achieve this without a diverse base of investors/partners. Invest time and energy in creating and maintaining relationships with different types of investors/partners – the returns are undoubtedly worth it. These relationships can open up doors for you, introduce you to new capital structures and tools, enhance your credibility in the real estate space, and impart useful knowledge and skills. Thus, the best thing you can do to further your business is to earn the trust (and repeat business) of your investors with consistent communication and outstanding performance.

Good sponsors are long-term thinkers. Real estate assets are often bought, developed and sold within 5 to 10 years, but relationships remain rewarding for far longer. So don't just invest in property, invest in people too.

If you're interested in investing or partnering as an LP / co-GP / JV partner with us at Lone Star Capital, please click here[7] to learn more. To stay up to date with monthly newsletters from me, which include new articles on multifamily investing, real estate finance, and more, sign up here[8]. Finally, if you enjoyed this book, I would greatly appreciate a review on Amazon to help spread the word.

[7] Learn more about investing/partnering with Lone Star Capital here: https://lscre.com/invest-with-us.

[8] Sign up for our newsletter here: www.lscre.com

ABOUT THE AUTHOR

Rob Beardsley oversees acquisitions and capital markets for Lone Star Capital and has acquired over $300M of multifamily real estate. He has evaluated thousands of opportunities using proprietary underwriting models and published the number one book on multifamily underwriting, The Definitive Guide to Underwriting Multifamily Acquisitions.

Made in the USA
Las Vegas, NV
02 July 2024

91738036R00066